Taoist Feng Shui

Taoist
Feng Shui

SUSAN LEVITT

Destiny Books
Rochester, Vermont

Dedicated to Professor Takeko Stover, who opened the door to 10,000 things.

Destiny Books
One Park Street
Rochester, Vermont 05767
www.InnerTraditions.com

Destiny Books is a division of Inner Traditions International

Library of Congress Cataloging-in-Publication Data
Levitt, Susan.
    Taoist feng shui : the ancient roots of the Chinese art of placement / Susan Levitt.
    p. cm.
    ISBN 0-89281-723-2 (alk. paper)
    1. Feng-shui. 2. Taoism. I. Title.

BF1779.F4 L46 1999
133.3'337—dc21   99-054415

Printed and bound in Canada

10 9 8 7 6 5 4 3 2 1

Text design and layout by Virginia Scott
This book was typeset in Berkeley Book

What is Tao?

There was something formless and perfect
before the universe was born.
It is serene. Empty.
Solitary. Unchanging.
Infinite. Eternally present.
It is the mother of the universe.
For lack of a better name, I call it the Tao.

It flows through all things,
inside and outside, and returns
to the orgin of all things.
The Tao is great.
The universe is great.
Earth is great.
Each human is great.

These are the four great powers.
A human follows the earth.
Earth follows the universe.
The universe follows the Tao.
The Tao follows only itself.

Contents

Foreword

INSIGHT, INTUITION, AND THE ABILITY TO OBSERVE NATURE are essential for understanding the intimate interplay between the energies of people and place. Universal principles underlying timeless wisdom are always waiting to be discovered, if only we are willing to pay attention, and open our minds and hearts to the feelings and sensations that surround us, particularly those from our living and working environments.

Long ago in ancient China, the sage rulers developed a conceptual system to understand and explain how the spaces we inhabit affect our lives. Their forms, location, orientation, color, characteristics, design, and arrangement all play critical roles in what came to be feng shui, the science and art of placement.

Along with destiny and luck, feng shui exerts a powerful, almost all-encompassing influence on the course of our lives. With feng shui we are able to work directly with and even transform *chi*, the basic energy that underlies all life, to overcome obstacles, create prosperity, and bring us into balance with ourselves and the world around us.

As with any path to greater understanding, unless we find an entry and gain access to even the simplest of its truths, it will serve little practical use no matter what its intrinsic value may be. We can all thank Susan Levitt for her excellent job of presenting the Taoist approach to feng shui in an eminently clear and thorough fashion. Translating ancient ideas and practices in a way that lets us apply them to our busy and often overcomplicated modern lives is no easy task, let alone achieving a seamless integration between theory and practical examples.

I first met Susan when she invited me to analyze the feng shui of her Sausalito home. Captivated by the opportunity to expand her Taoist studies into a new arena, and incorporate feng shui with her practice as a Chinese astrologer, she accompanied me on a series of appointments arranged with her astrology clients. From the very first session her zeal and acumen were inspiring, as there is nothing a teacher enjoys so much as a dedicated student, particularly one who brings such unique gifts and talents. She continued with professional training as a consultant, studied with Grand Master Lin Yun, and now has achieved the distinction of reintegrating modern feng shui with its Taoist roots.

I wish you the best of success applying the practical wisdom contained within the pages of *Taoist Feng Shui,* and urge you to follow Susan's example. Like the ancient Taoist sages, investigate, observe, explore, and add your special insights and discoveries to the wealth of techniques and methods for transforming life with feng shui. Together we can create places filled with balance and harmony, for ourselves and the generations yet to come.

Seann Xenja

Acknowledgments

THANKS TO His Holiness Grand Master Lin Yun Rinpoche, a Monkey, wise trickster, and holy being, and feng shui educator Seann Xenja, a brave white Tiger. The purity of their souls is a great inspiration. Thanks also to my sister Char Levitt, a Dog strong and true, and my sister-in-law, Nadine Greiner, a mighty Dragon. Their love and guidance are my most treasured gifts.

ONE

History of the Dragon

EVERYWHERE ON OUR PLANET—from the pyramids in Egypt to the monoliths of Stonehenge in England to the Ming tombs in China—ancient people honored sacred places. Unique mountains, rivers, hills, and groves, or places where natural phenomena occurred, such as geysers and volcanoes, were sacred places.

Feng shui (pronounced "fung shway") is the ancient Chinese art and science of locating a sacred place on earth. The literal translation of *feng shui* is "wind" and "water," two elements of nature. The ancient Chinese people developed feng shui based on their unique spiritual view of the world. They studied nature to make sense of the universe. In nature they sensed *chi* energy, the breath of life in all things. They understood the harmony of life by observing nature. By recognizing chi in a landscape, the ancient ones determined which locations would be safe from danger, provide lush vegetation, or harmoniously align with the geomagnetism of the earth. Through observation of natural forces, the Chinese invented the magnetic compass. Feng shui is also based on compass directions and astronomical patterns.

The philosophy of the balance of nature became the religion of Taoism (pronounced "Dowism"). Priests of Taoism, who were both female and male, discovered and developed feng shui geomancy through observation of landforms, river flows, the movement of planets, the behavior of animals, and changing weather conditions. When to cultivate crops, how to irrigate with the flooding rivers, and where to construct buildings and tombs were feng

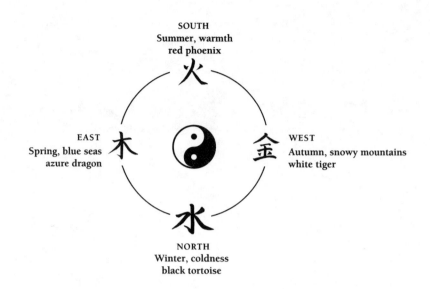

SOUTH
Summer, warmth
red phoenix

EAST
Spring, blue seas
azure dragon

WEST
Autumn, snowy mountains
white tiger

NORTH
Winter, coldness
black tortoise

shui concerns of the early Taoists. China is a vast and geographically varied country. The many ways to interpret chi in a landscape are specific to each environment. Certain land formations were named after animals, such as the azure dragon, white tiger, red phoenix, and black turtle. These vivid animal metaphors describe different types of chi.

The ancient Taoists observed that we humans live where earth meets heaven, between these two great forces in the "Middle Kingdom." In the Northern Hemisphere of the Middle Kingdom, we receive warmth, heat, and vitality from the south. South is located at the top of the Chinese compass. Its symbolic animal is the red phoenix, which represents beauty and goodness. From the north comes winter cold, snow, and darkness. North is located at the bottom of the compass. North's symbolic animal is the black tortoise, which represents long life and endurance. The direction east corresponds to springtime, blue seas, and new growth. East's symbolic animal is the azure dragon, which represents majesty and magnificence. The direction west corresponds to autumn and snowy mountains. West's symbolic animal is the white tiger, which exemplifies bravery and strength.

Taoist observation of nature concluded that curved, flowing lines slow chi and bring abundance. Harmonious chi moves in a curved, graceful line, as if following the natural course of a river. Sharp, straight lines bring *sha* chi, or bad chi. An example of architecture that avoids straight lines is the Great Wall of China, first constructed during the Qin dynasty (221–206 B.C.). The massive wall winds through the countryside along the ridges of mountain chains known as the "dragon's veins." The landform of a mountain is symbolized by a dragon. Hills, ridges, and mountains are all shapes through which the dragon's blood (chi) circulates. Watercourses are the ducts through which more chi can flow. If there are too many channels, the chi is dispersed and weakened. The higher the concentration of chi in the dragon's veins, the greater the harmony of an area. An ideal dragon's lair is a hollow well protected on three sides.

The dragon symbol may seem odd to westerners. In the West, the dragon is a hideous beast who personifies the worst moral qualities. But in Asian cultures, the qualities of the dragon are the opposite of European interpretations. The dragon is not an evil, malefic enemy. Instead, the mighty and magnificent dragon symbolizes royalty, prosperity, wisdom, and benevolence. The dragon was the most sacred mystical animal throughout thousands of years of Chinese history and was even associated with imperial majesty. For example, the chair a Chinese emperor sat on was referred to as the "dragon chair," and the robe a Chinese emperor wore was called the "dragon robe."

In a landscape, a large dragon mountain is complemented by a smaller hill. This smaller hill is symbolized by a tiger. An old Chinese way of describing where the dragon meets the tiger is to compare the site to the upper and lower portions of a human arm. In the elbow bend of the arm is the best place for luck and harmony, for within this horseshoe shape is the best natural collection of chi. Regardless of compass direction, the dragon side is located on the left-hand side when looking out from (not facing) the front of a building. The tiger side is on the right.

The famous burial place of Chinese royalty, the Ming tombs northwest of Beijing, was built according to classic dragon and tiger harmony. The Tianshoushan hills behind the tombs are a natural barrier against harmful forces brought by winds. The beautiful landscape includes gentle streams that run in front of the tombs. The Ming tombs to the east are on the Azure Dragon Hill, and the tombs to the west are on the White Tiger Hill. The emperor's tomb was, of course, placed in the center of the horseshoe shape. The other royal graves were scattered in harmonious locations among the hills. This dragon and tiger harmony is seen all over the world where indigenous people follow geomantic earth patterns. For example, the Mesoamerican cities of present-day Los Angeles and Guadalajara exist in dragon and tiger junctures.

The spiritual importance of the ancestral tradition is a key feature of classic feng shui. A correct burial site that is balanced in the landscape promotes the ancestor's ability to aid the living. The ancestors and the land they inhabited create a continuous link to modern humanity. This may seem like an unusual concept to westerners, especially those Americans whose ancestral lands are on the other side of the world. But the benevolence of ancestors is a cardinal aspect of many ancient traditions. Countless generations developed the traditions of guardianship of the landscape in which those ancestral spirits are located. In Chinese ghost stories and legends, an unhappy corpse haunts the living until his burial site is corrected. Then he can rest in peace for all eternity.

Northern Chinese culture originated along the banks of the Huang Ho (Yellow) River during the first Chinese dynasty of the Bronze Age, the Shang dynasty (ca. 1766–1122 B.C.). The ancient Shang people created a pictographic script with which to express abstract ideas. Archeologists have unearthed inscribed bones that were used for divination, indicating the spiritual and mystical values of the Shang times.

About 1122 B.C. the Shangs were overthrown by the Zhous, who established their own dynasty (1122–221 B.C.). Political trouble and social unrest existed at the end of the Zhou dynasty, and the empire declined as the result of warring among the states within the Zhou feudal system. But the Zhou dynasty was also a time of great intellectual and artistic ferment. Feng shui was documented as early as 960 B.C., and a great flowering of feng shui took place during 770–475 B.C. under Zhou rulership. Taoist philosophers from the late Zhou period (600–221 B.C.) include Lao-tzu (ca. 604–531 B.C.), author of the *Tao Te Ching,* and Mo Ti (born ca. 500 B.C.), the teacher of universal love. The third great Zhou philosopher was Confucius (ca. 551–479 B.C.). The philosophies of Taoism, Confucianism, and Buddhism (which came to China from India in the year A.D. 68) formed Chinese culture and influenced feng shui development.

Another great flowering of feng shui occurred during the Han dynasty (206 B.C.–A.D. 220). The expansion of the mighty Chinese empire during the Han dynasty incorporated myriad geographical zones and climates, each with their own feng shui needs. Feng shui progressed further during the great empire of the Tang dynasty (A.D. 618–907) and the artistic Song dynasties of the northern Song (A.D. 960–1126) and the southern Song (A.D. 1127–1279), which have been compared to the Renaissance.

Ming translates as "brilliant," and cultural advancements made during the Ming dynasty (A.D. 1368–1644) were brilliant indeed. The Ming emperor Chu Yuan-chang reunited China by capturing Beijing in 1368 and released China from the one-hundred-year rule of the Mongols. Chu Yuan-chang revitalized the feng shui wisdom of the Han dynasty "Canon of Dwellings" to create his beautiful and peaceful burial site, the Ming tombs. According to the rules of the canon, his site is protected from the dominant northern winds, and the view is of continuous mountains—clefts or passages are not seen between them, and they are of auspicious shapes. Modern feng shui geomancers enhanced the peace and harmony of the Ming tombs during the Great Leap Forward (1958–1959). A water reservoir built to the south added a lovely view. In this way, continuous peace is maintained between heaven and earth.

TWO

The Way of the Tao

ACCORDING TO THE TAOISTS, all energy is interconnected. This connection, the Tao, is symbolized by the familiar image known as yin and yang. Traditionally, yin is the dark, feminine, and receptive principle, and yang is the light, masculine, and active principle. Together, yin and yang flow endlessly into each other. Each creates and defines the other's opposite. Yin and yang are understood relative to each other and are in a con-

stant state of flux. For example, because of the existence of dark, the concept of light has meaning. Similarly, high is defined by low, and sweet is defined by sour. In Western thought, the balance of yin and yang could be interpreted as conflicting opposites, yet in Taoist thought there is no duality.

Even today yin and yang remain the natural order of the universe because the yin and yang cycle repeats endlessly. High noon, the most yang hour, progresses to midnight, the most yin hour. The summer solstice, the longest day, is the most yang time of the year. It gives way to winter solstice, the longest night, which is the most yin. Even in our bodies we experience the endless dance of yin and yang. When we inhale, our lungs expand to the most yang point, and when we exhale they contract to the most yin point. At the height of yang, yin ascends and yang declines. At the height of yin, yang ascends and yin declines. Death occurs when yin and yang separate.

Here is a partial list of the many qualities of yin and yang:

YIN	YANG
earth	heaven
valley	mountain
cyclic	linear
black	white
dark	light
female	male
moon	sun
water	fire
wet	dry
cold	hot
slow	fast
passive	active
receptive	assertive
round	angular
smooth	rough

One interpretation of yin and yang in a landscape is that mountains are yang, and valleys are yin. In architecture yin buildings house the dead, and yang buildings house the living. Yin and yang balance also applies to interior spaces. An excessively yin room is dark, damp, and poorly lit. Such an environment can evoke feelings of sadness. An excessively yang room is too bright. It can bring on feelings of anxiety. When balanced, yin and yang are appropriately applied to interior spaces. A bedroom is a quiet yin room for sleep, while a living room is a yang room for lively conversation and activity—for living.

The interplay of yin and yang is described in the verses of the Taoist philosopher Lao-tzu, who distilled Taoist wisdom into eighty-one short chapters of verse in his classic book, the *Tao Te Ching*. He explains the harmonious yet dualistic principles of the Tao:

> *Thirty spokes join together in a single wheel,*
> *but it is the center hole*

that makes the wagon move.
We shape a lump of clay into a vessel,
but it is the emptiness inside the vessel
that makes it useful.

We hammer doors and windows of wood for a house,
but it is the empty inner space
that makes the rooms livable.

We build with the tangible,
but the intangible is what we use.

THREE

Eight Trigrams

CHI IN A LANDSCAPE CAN BE DISCERNED by observing landforms and sensing the balance of yin and yang, but to gather more information about a specific site, a feng shui compass is used. The inner ring of the feng shui compass comprises eight trigrams. A trigram is a symbol made up of three stacked lines. A solid line represents yang chi, and a broken line represents yin chi. The eight trigrams in Chinese are *ba-gua,* pronounced "bah gwah." "Ba" means "eight," and "gua" means "trigram." The next chapter will explain how to apply the ba-gua to a room, building, site, and landscape. A basic understanding of the eight trigrams is helpful because they are important reference points in the application of feng shui.

The creation of the eight trigrams is attributed to the legendary Chinese king Fu Xi, a ruler during the ancient Neolithic period of the third millennium B.C. This pre–Shang dynasty culture was surprisingly well developed, as evidenced by the archeological excavations at An-yang in northern China. Ruler Fu Xi devised the eight trigrams through Taoist observation of the natural world as seen on the patterns of a tortoise's shell as the animal emerged from the Yellow River. Fu Xi saw the microcosmos of the primal energies of the universe symbolized in the eight orderly markings of the tortoise's shell.

The eight tortoise shell markings became the eight trigrams, which symbolize the natural world as Heaven, Earth, Fire, Water, Mountain, Lake, Wind, and Thunder. Fu Xi laid out these eight symbols in an eight-sided map that became the ba-gua, similar to a tortoise shell in shape. His arrangement

9

is referred to as the "early Heaven" sequence. The eight trigrams were restudied and brought to prominence in the Chinese imperial court by King Wen, the founder of the Zhou dynasty. King Wen wrote extensively about the eight trigrams in what became the "later Heaven" sequence. It is the ba-gua arrangement of King Wen that is used today as an important feng shui tool.

The following diagram shows how the eight trigrams are born from yin and yang. The top image is the symbol of the Tao, the balance of yin and yang. A solid line represents yang chi and a broken line represents yin chi.

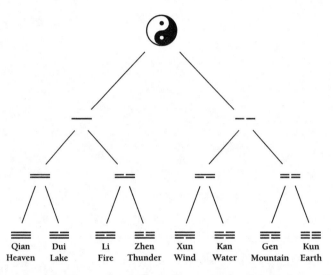

| Qian | Dui | Li | Zhen | Xun | Kan | Gen | Kun |
| Heaven | Lake | Fire | Thunder | Wind | Water | Mountain | Earth |

The four combinations of two lines illustrate the four seasons. Two solid lines represent *tai* yang, or summer—the great male principle, a symbol of the sun and heat. A solid yang line under a broken yin line indicates *shao* yin, or springtime—the lesser male principle, a symbol of the moon and cold. A broken yin line under a solid yang line stands for shao yang, or autumn—the lesser female principle, a symbol of the stars and daylight. And two broken yin lines epitomize tai yin, or winter—the great female principle, a symbol of the planets and night.

From Taoist philosophy comes the inspiration to combine yin lines and yang lines to create a trigram. As Lao-tzu states in the *Tao Te Ching*:

> *The Tao gives to One.*
> *One gives birth to Two.*

Two gives birth to Three.

Three gives birth to ten thousand things.

Understanding the eight trigrams opens the door to understanding Taoist feng shui. It is in the application of the ba-gua that we create order and harmony. Please memorize these eight trigrams to simplify your feng shui practice. They will be referred to throughout the book.

☰ Heaven

Heaven's trigram is composed of solid yang lines because Heaven is strong and undivided and is most yang, the great male principle. Heaven represents the celestial forces generating "ten thousand things." It is the creative source, perfection, strength, vitality, originality, and power. All things are properly ordered: the sun shines, rain falls, and people prosper. Through strength of character and fortitude, obstacles are overcome.

☷ Earth

Earth's trigram is composed of three broken yin lines because Earth is open and receptive—to rain, sun, and other natural forces—and is most yin. Earth is the complement to Heaven. Earth represents the great female principle from which ten thousand things are nurtured, the femininity of Mother Earth, the receptive and yielding principle. Performing good deeds with gracious acceptance results in the enjoyment of abundant good fortune. To be virtuous and loving will fulfill one's destiny.

☳ Thunder

Thunder's trigram is composed of a solid yang line below two broken yin lines, because thunder hits solidly and rises to disperse. Thunder represents dynamic movement, activity, vitality, development, and growth. Thunder is for agitating ten thousand things, and nothing is swifter than Thunder.

Thunder's loud boom may frighten or intimidate, but it can inspire people to change and improve their character. Do not act when frightened; instead, cultivate patience. Difficulties can be opportunities for future development.

☵ Water

Water's trigram is composed of broken yin lines at the bottom and top with a solid yang line in the center. Water may seem clear and uniform, but it has a solid mass in the center. A wave will crash when the surface of the water moves at a faster rate than the solid central mass. Water is for moistening ten thousand things; nothing is more humid than Water. Water represents mystery, profound meaning, and possible danger. One will not drown if she believes in her ability to prevail.

☶ Mountain

Mountain's trigram is composed of two broken yin lines below a solid yang line. Under the solid top is a space, indicating a cave inside the mountain. Mountains are for bringing ten thousand things to conclusion and gain. Nothing is more perfect than Mountain. Huge, immovable Mountain represents meditation, movement halted, and resting of the body, mind, and spirit. There is great value in remaining still and contemplating actions. Exercising restraint brings success.

☴ Wind

Wind's trigram is composed of a broken yin line below two solid yang lines. The strength of Wind is shown by the two solid yang lines in the Middle Kingdom and heaven over the broken yin line of the earth below. The open space is like a crevice for the wind to penetrate. Wind is for twirling ten thousand things, and nothing is more effective than Wind. Success can be achieved through yielding to superior forces and new opportunities. Wind represents pliability, penetration, influence from others, and flexibility. Maintain integrity and awareness to avoid being swayed or blown in the wrong direction.

☲ Fire

Fire's trigram is composed of solid yang lines at the bottom and top with a broken yin line in the middle. Like a flame, fire appears to take form, but its core is empty. Fire is for drying up ten thousand things—nothing is more drying than Fire. Allow knowledge and wisdom to shine as a bright flame to ensure and maintain good fortune. Take care of those less able and cultivate a demeanor of respect. Fire represents expansion, ideas, illumination, clarity, brilliance, and beauty.

☱ Lake

Lake's trigram is composed of two solid yang lines below one broken yin line. A lake is open and receptive on the surface, yet contains mass below (unlike Water, which is open at the bottom to create running water). Lake is for satisfying ten thousand things; nothing is more gratifying than Lake. Happiness is spread by praising the virtues of others and encouraging their development. Avoid pursuing superficial pleasures. Lake represents joy, happiness, pleasure, contentment, and possible excess.

The eight trigrams exist symbolically in our own bodies. They are the basis of acupuncture meridian theory in traditional Chinese medicine. Heaven symbolizes the body's master channel, which runs up the spine (the yang channel to heaven). Lake is represented by the lungs and the large intestines, Fire by the heart and the small intestines, Thunder by the pericardium (the membranous sac around the heart) and the "triple burner" (which regulates body heat), Wind by the liver and the gallbladder, Water by the kidneys and the urinary bladder, and Mountain by the stomach and the spleen. The conception and confluence of all yin channels of the body exemplify Earth.

FOUR

Ba-Gua Map

KING WEN'S SEQUENCE of the eight trigrams, the ba-gua, creates an eight-sided map, or template, to place over rooms, buildings, sites, and landscapes. Each gua corresponds to one of eight areas of life experience: career and journey, knowledge and self-awareness, helpful people and travel, family and health, children and creativity, wealth and prosperity, fame and reputation, and relationships and marriage.

By using a simple compass, you can determine the location of each area of life experience. Then you can balance or enhance an area of life experience that is lacking in quality and satisfaction. The ba-gua directions, with corresponding life experiences, are given in the chart on page 15.

If you hold a compass and find exact south, the direction of the red phoenix, that is the gua that corresponds to the element fire, which represents fame, personal reputation, and how others perceive you. The fire location is at the southernmost point of your room, building, or lot. In a room, this is the spot to place candles. In a building, it is the ideal position for a fireplace. In a lot, this is the location for outdoor lights.

There is another method of applying King Wen's ba-gua, taught by the feng shui expert His Holiness Lin Yun Grand Master Rinpoche. He aligns the ba-gua with the main entrance or most-used entryway of a room, building, or the front of a lot; this main entrance is called the "mouth of chi." By placing the ba-gua map on the mouth of chi, all guas can be located without the use of a compass. In this way, the ba-gua map is ever changing, because the guas shift

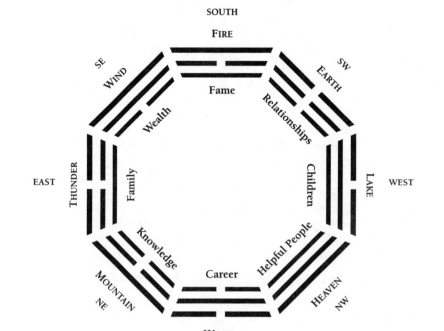

position depending on the location of the mouth of chi. I have found that realigning the ba-gua for each room and the overall lot brings excellent results.

At first, it may be challenging to determine the mouth of chi and move the ba-gua map accordingly, instead of just applying the compass directions. To help you learn, the specific instructions in this book refer to the changing ba-gua, but the basic information can also be used with the compass system.

Most important to remember is the fact that the ba-gua map changes position depending on the entrance. This mouth of chi entryway will be in the Mountain/knowledge, Water/career, or Heaven/helpful people area of the ba-gua, depending on the location of the doorway on the wall. When entering a room, the Fire/fame area is directly across from you. (This differs from the compass application, where Fire/fame is in the south.) The Earth/relationship area is in the far right corner. The Wind/wealth area is in the far left corner. The Lake/children area is on the wall to your right. The Thunder/family area is on

THE EVER-CHANGING BA-GUA DIAGRAM

Xun WIND wealth prosperity	Li FIRE fame reputation	Kun EARTH relationships marriage
Zhen THUNDER family health	TAO center	Dui LAKE children creativity
Gen MOUNTAIN knowledge self-awareness	Kan WATER career journey	Qian HEAVEN helpful people travel

MOUTH OF CHI

DOOR IN
MOUNTAIN/KNOWLEDGE

DOOR IN
WATER/CAREER

DOOR IN
HEAVEN/HELPFUL PEOPLE

Entry will be in one of these three locations.

the wall to your left. The Heaven/helpful people area is in the near corner to your right. The Mountain/knowledge area is in the corner to your near left. The Water/career area is the middle of the wall that holds the entrance.

This layout also applies on a larger scale. When entering the front door of a building, the Fire/fame area is the room farthest away from the front door, at the back of the entire building. The other areas line up accordingly. When considering a lot or property, the Fire/fame area is the center of the backyard.

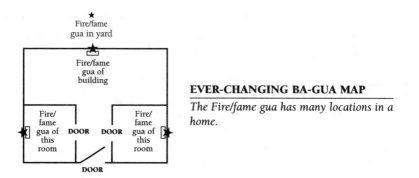

★
Fire/fame
gua in yard

Fire/fame
gua of
building

Fire/
fame
gua of
this
room

DOOR **DOOR**

Fire/
fame
gua of
this
room

DOOR

EVER-CHANGING BA-GUA MAP

The Fire/fame gua has many locations in a home.

When placing the map over a landscape, the Fire/fame area is the center point farthest way. To enhance the Fire/fame area of your life, attention should be given to every Fire/fame gua on the lot, in the building, and in each room, especially the living room.

When placing the ba-gua map over a lot, building, or room, you may find a projection or extra space such as an additional room or patio. This will add to the power of the gua that has the projection. But if an area is missing or incomplete on the ba-gua map, what is missing will lack chi. A missing area needs to be enhanced to create balance and give it more energy.

PROJECTIONS AND MISSING AREAS

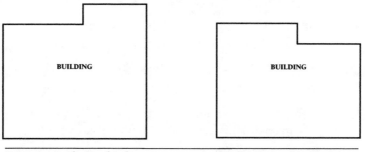

BUILDING

BUILDING

Projection in the Earth/rela-tionship gua

Earth/relationship gua is missing

The Water/career position corresponds to one's career or profession, or journey through life. It defines how we flow in the river of life and make a positive contribution through our good work. If one has difficulties with a career or is not engaged in what is his or her true calling, enhancement of this area of the ba-gua in the workplace and home may help bring transformation. If this area is incomplete or missing in a room, building, or lot, there may be career frustration. If it is larger or if there is a projection, it suggests abundance.

The Mountain/knowledge position corresponds to knowledge and self-awareness. When we cultivate self-awareness, we can be solid, secure, and as immovable as a mountain. Attention paid to this area of the ba-gua enhances spiritual development. In modern society, the value of meditation, contemplation, and reflection is overlooked, yet so many personal and social problems would be solved with focused attention on this area. If this area is incomplete or missing, a lack of sensitivity and awareness results, and it may be difficult to conceive a child. If this area is larger or if there is an enhancement, wisdom is easily attained.

The Thunder/family position corresponds to family and ancestors. As thunder precedes a storm, our ancestors precede us. This area also corresponds to health, since many illnesses are genetic; they "run in the family." Conscientious attention to this area can transform conflicting family relationships to experiences of gratitude, respect, and appreciation for our parents, ancestors, and teachers. This area also corresponds to the balance of power with bosses and managers at work. If this area is incomplete or missing, there may be a lack of physical endurance and stamina. If it is larger or if there is a projection, success is indicated.

The Wind/wealth position corresponds to wealth, prosperity, and blessings, as if good fortune arrived on gentle winds. The gifts from this area are wealth, prosperity, harmony, abundance, honors, and promotion. Development of the Wind position can increase opportunities for making and receiving money, expanding a business, and good luck. If this area is incomplete or missing, there may be difficulties with money management, legal affairs, contracts, taxes, and lack of money. If this area is larger or if there is a projection, good luck is indicated.

The Fire/fame position corresponds to fame, reputation, and respect from others. Bright fire attracts, like a flame for a moth, and can illuminate the way for others. Improvements to this area can bring recognition of one's achievements, prominence, clarity, and fulfillment of purpose. If this area is incomplete or missing, there may be lack of confidence or the need to seek approval. If this area is larger or if there is a projection, one may become known in society or can achieve self-realization.

The Earth/relationship position corresponds to relationships and marriage. Earth is the receptive and nurturing feminine principle, so we, too, must be open, receptive, and nurturing to sustain harmonious relationships. Improvements to this area can create more fulfilling relationships, both romantic and platonic, and increase social activities. If this area is incomplete or missing, one may feel lonely or unloved, and women in particular may be uncomfortable in the home. If this area is larger or if there is a projection, relationships will be fulfilling and plentiful, and women will be more content.

The Lake/children position corresponds to children and creativity. Like innocent children playing and swimming safely at a peaceful lake, we can return to our childlike awe to see the amazing world around us. Development of this area encourages one to freely share his or her creative self-expression and demonstrate wisdom to compassionately guide children as they grow. If this area is incomplete or missing, one may feel blocked in expressing creativity or will not be able to save money to spend on enjoyment. If this area is larger or if there is a projection, it indicates youthfulness, creativity, joy, imagination, and sociability.

The Heaven/helpful people position corresponds to those who assist us in life as if they were angels sent from heaven. This gua also corresponds to opportunities for travel. Enhancements to this area can encourage philanthropy, networking, reciprocity in relationships, volunteers, helpful friends, qualified staff, good neighbors, and the ability to find others to assist you when needed. If this area is incomplete or missing, there may be illness, difficulties with employers, and lack of vitality. If this area is larger or if there is a projection, it brings empathy and concern for the less fortunate.

It is in the balance of all eight guas that we find harmony, peace, and contentment. Each gua does not exist in isolation from the others. There is a reciprocity between all areas of life experience. For example, the Earth/relationship gua must be enhanced if a marriage partner is desired, but it is also important to develop Mountain/knowledge. If you know yourself, you can create a strong relationship with another. If the Wind/wealth gua is abundant in your life, give to others to become their Heaven/helpful person. In our modern materialistic society, people want to rapidly develop their Wind/wealth gua. If other areas of the ba-gua are not developed along with it, imbalance will result. As the Taoist master Lao-tzu explains:

> *Fill a bowl to the brim*
> *and the contents will spill.*
> *Keep beating and sharpening a sword*
> *and the edge will not stay sharp for long.*
> *Fill your house with gold and jade*
> *and it can no longer be guarded.*

FIVE

Five Elements

TAOIST COSMOLOGY IS STRUCTURED on five natural elements: fire, earth, metal, water, and wood. These five Taoist elements are also translated as the five powers, five virtues, five phases, or five changing elements. On a metaphysical level, the five elements are not really tangible substances, but five different representations of chi. Everything on earth and in heaven is characterized by the constant interplay among the five elements, which are always moving, unstable, and changeable, like the dance of yin and yang.

The Taoist concept of the five elements can be traced back as far as the Yellow Emperor Huang-Ti (twenty-seventh century B.C.), considered the ancestor of the Chinese people. According to legend, he lived for 117 years and ruled peaceably for one hundred years. The *Huang Ti Nei Jing*, known in English as *The Yellow Emperor's Classic of Internal Medicine,* the world's oldest medical textbook, explains how health can be achieved and maintained by the correct balance of the five elements.

Each element possesses distinct characteristics and can exist in either a yang or a yin state.

 Fire

The element fire is the most masculine of the five elements and is considered very yang. When fire expresses masculine yang energy, its color is red, and it is symbolized by burning wood. When fire expresses feminine yin energy, its color is purple, and it is symbolized by the flame of a lamp, small and contained, yet helpful.

Fire's planet is Mars, the intense red planet. Fire's season is summer, the time of heat, growth, warmth, and increased light. Fire's direction is south, and its climate is hot. The feng shui building shape of fire is a pointed roof (A-frame), especially row apartments with pointed roofs. Fire's landscape form is a peaked mountain. The pointed peaks of mountains and roofs are similar in shape to a flame. The fire room of a home is the living room, where much activity takes place. Fire corresponds to the three Taoist astrological signs of summertime: Serpent (May), Horse (June), and Sheep (July). Fire's symbol is a red phoenix.

Feng shui fire objects in a home or office are all types of lighting devices, including electric lights and lamps, candles, oil lamps, natural sunlight, and fireplaces. Fluorescent bulbs deplete chi, whereas full-spectrum light bulbs attract and maintain good chi. Wild animals and domesticated pets represent fire. Animal parts, such as feathers, fur, wool, and bone, are also considered to belong to the element fire. Visual art that depicts fire, sunshine, or animals symbolizes fire, as do red colors, including purple, scarlet, magenta, hot pink, and orange.

You are a fire personality type if your year of birth ends in the number six or seven. Red years (yang fire) end in the number six: 1906, 1916, 1926, 1936, 1946, 1956, 1966, 1976, 1986, 1996, 2006, 2016, and so on. Purple years (yin fire) end in the number seven: 1907, 1917, 1927, 1937, 1947, 1957, 1967, 1977, 1987, 1997, 2007, 2017, and so on. (Refer to the appendix for exact dates for those born in late January and early February.) You could also be a fire type if you have much of the fire element in your physical constitution. This can be determined through pulse diagnosis by a doctor of traditional Chinese medicine. The home environment of a fire personality type showcases different types of objects. Fire types are eclectic individuals who enjoy decorating with unique art pieces. Their very interesting homes and offices are places to display their treasures from around the world.

Fire character traits are love, passion, leadership, spirituality, insight, dynamism, aggression, intuition, reason, and expressiveness. The fire personality is direct—right out front. Fire types are funny, eclectic, and impulsive people, but they can be scattered. They must not indulge in the unpleasant personality trait of excessive arrogance. Instead, they succeed by becoming warmhearted and generous. Experiences of love, compassion, fun, joy, and pleasure are healing for fire individuals. The challenge for a fire type is to share joy and laughter without thought of reward. The emotion of happiness is associated with the element fire. Other fire emotions include excitement, joy, vanity, jealousy, frustration, regret, grief from loss of love, and disappointment in relationships.

In traditional Chinese medicine, fire's body organs are the heart and the small intestines. For this reason, a fire personality may have a predisposition to heart problems, such as heart attacks, or may experience minor digestive problems in the small intestines. The element wood nurtures the element fire; wood's body organ is the liver. Fire types must avoid alcoholic beverages that heat (overstimulate) the liver. Liver excess is a false way to empower the heart and causes an imbalance between fire and wood. A red yang fire type is extremely resilient and can miraculously overcome most illnesses. A purple yin fire type may develop a weak heart owing to emotional stress. Heart illness and fire imbalance can often be read in the face: a cleft in the tip of the nose or a complexion that is too red.

FIRE

Colors: red (yang) and purple (yin)
Building shape: pointed roof (A-frame), especially pointed-roof row apartments
Landscape form: peaked mountain
Home environment: many different types of objects
Room: living room
Taoist astrological signs: Serpent, Horse, Sheep
Planet: Mars
Direction: south
Climate: hot
Season: summer
Emotions: happiness and love when balanced, excitement when imbalanced
Symbol: red phoenix
Body organs: heart (yin) and small intestines (yang)

土 Earth

The element earth is yin—feminine, like Mother Earth in the West. When earth expresses masculine yang energy, its color is yellow, and it is symbolized by a hill. When earth expresses feminine yin energy, its color is gold, and it is symbolized by a valley.

Earth's planet is Saturn, and its climate is damp. Earth's "season" is the last eighteen days of each of the four seasons, the time of transition. Earth's location (direction) is at the center. The feng shui building shape of earth is a flat roof and a square or oblong structure. Estates and low, heavy houses that have stood for centuries are also earth structures. Earth's landscape form is a small mountain with a flat, tabletop peak. An example of an earth mountain in America is the mesa of the Southwest. The earth room of a home is the dining room, where eating takes place. Earth corresponds to all twelve Taoist astrological signs. Earth's symbol is the black-and-white yin/yang symbol.

Earth objects in a home or office environment are all types of earthenware containers and vases, ceramic pieces, clay tiles, bricks, and adobe. Visual art that depicts earthy landscapes, such as fields and natural environments, represents earth, as do all yellow colors, including ochre and gold.

You are an earth personality type if your year of birth ends in the number eight or nine. Yellow years (yang earth) end in the number eight: 1908, 1918, 1928, 1938, 1948, 1958, 1968, 1978, 1988, 1998, 2008, 2018, and so on. Gold years (yin earth) end in the number nine: 1909, 1919, 1929, 1939, 1949, 1959, 1969, 1979, 1989, 1999, 2009, 2019, and so forth. (Refer to the appendix for exact dates for those born in late January and early February.) You could also be an earth type if you have much of the earth element in your physical constitution. This can be determined through pulse diagnosis by a doctor of traditional Chinese medicine.

The home environment of an earth personality type is very comfortable. Earth personality types love a cozy home and are not content if comfort is lacking. Thick rugs, stuffed furniture, and fancy or ornate decorative elements are found in the typical earth residence. Such homes are often very inviting, and guests do not want to leave. Earth types tend to collect too many objects and create clutter. When imbalanced, an earth personality collects and hoards excessively, acquiring material goods to create a sense of security. In these instances, clutter must be reduced.

Earth character traits are stability, practicality, reliability, industriousness, empathy, honesty, kindness, and prudence. Earth types value friendship. They are kind, nurturing, and grounded people. Earth individuals do well to meditate and nourish themselves physically, emotionally, and spiritually. They must learn to develop clear boundaries and take care of themselves. The challenge for earth types is to honor their sympathetic nature and experience empathy with others. The emotion of sympathy is associated with the element earth. Other earth traits are pensiveness, worry, thoughtfulness, instinctive awareness, and reflection. Just as one takes in nutrients through the stomach, one assimilates life experiences through the element earth. A strong earth element helps us digest and accept fate and expand our circle of knowledge.

EARTH

Colors: yellow (yang) and gold (yin)

Building shape: flat roof, estates, and a square or oblong structure; also low, heavy houses that last for centuries

Landscape form: small mountain with flat, tabletop peak (mesa)

Home environment: very comfortable, but too many objects create clutter

Room: dining room

Taoist astrological signs: all twelve signs

Planet: Saturn

Direction: center

Climate: damp

Season: seasonal transition—the last eighteen days of the four seasons

Emotions: sympathy and instinctive awareness when balanced, worry when imbalanced

Symbol: yin/yang

Body organs: stomach (yang) and spleen (yin)

In traditional Chinese medicine, earth's body organs are the stomach and spleen (and the pancreas). Earth personalities should avoid foods that antagonize the stomach because they may have an inclination toward stomach disorders, such as ulcers or indigestion. A weak spleen can cause immune system problems owing to poor absorption of nutrients. Since a sweet taste is associated with the element earth, earth types could develop a sweet tooth. They must avoid the tendency to indulge in too many sweets and rich desserts. Stomach illness and earth imbalance are indicated as deep, sagging facial lines from the base of the nose to the outer corners of the lip.

 Metal

Metal is feminine because metal is extracted from the feminine earth (although metal is considered less feminine than earth or water). When metal expresses masculine yang energy, its color is white, and it is symbolized by a weapon. When metal expresses feminine yin energy, its color is silver, and it is symbolized by a kettle.

Metal's planet is Venus, and its season is autumn, the time of harvest (with a metal scythe), completion, and the beginning of rest. Metal's direction is west, and its climate is dry. The feng shui building shape of metal is a domed roof, especially in large domed buildings, or an arch. Very large properties also correspond to the element metal. Metal's landscape form is a lovely mountain with a gently curved peak, like a dome. The metal room of a home is the bedroom. Metal corresponds to the three Taoist astrological signs of fall: Monkey (August), Phoenix (September), and Dog (October). Metal's symbol is a white tiger.

Metal objects in a home or office are all objects or sculptures made of metal ores, whether silver, gold, brass, iron, aluminum, copper, tin, stainless steel, or metal alloys. Rocks, crystal, gems, and stones are also considered to be of the metal, not the earth, element. Visual art that is mostly white, silver, or light pastel in color represents metal.

You are a metal personality type if the year of your birth ends in the number zero or one. White years (yang metal) end in zero: 1900, 1910,

1920, 1930, 1940, 1950, 1960, 1970, 1980, 1990, 2000, 2010, 2020, and so forth. Silver years (yin metal) end in the number one: 1901, 1911, 1921, 1931, 1941, 1951, 1961, 1971, 1981, 1991, 2001, 2011, and so on. (Refer to the appendix for exact dates for those born in late January or early February.) You could also be a metal type if you have much of the metal element in your physical constitution. This can be determined through pulse diagnosis by a doctor of traditional Chinese medicine. Metal personality types strive to create order in their environment. The home or office of a metal personality type is a perfect, impeccable, and ordered room. Metal types prefer clean, minimalist design and dislike waste and excessive frilliness. "Form follows function" exemplifies the metal sensibility.

Metal character traits include strength, independence, focus, intensity, righteousness, and fluency in speech. The metal personality is very determined and powerful. Metal types are cool and reserved, with an aristocratic nature. They succeed by being less opinionated, accepting change, and gracefully releasing the past. The emotion of grief is associated with the element metal. Other metal emotions are gratitude, insecurity, inability to achieve parental or spousal expectations, and lack of confidence. The challenge for a metal type is to learn how to express grief and find healing.

METAL

Colors: white (yang) and silver (yin)

Building shape: dome roof, especially large domed buildings; arches; very large properties

Landscape form: lovely mountains with gently curved peaks

Home environment: a perfect, impeccable, and ordered room

Room: bedroom

Taoist astrological signs: Monkey, Phoenix, Dog

Planet: Venus

Direction: west

Climate: dry

Season: autumn

Emotions: gratitude when balanced, grief and insecurity when imbalanced

Symbol: white tiger

Body organs: lungs (yin) and large intestines (yang)

In traditional Chinese medicine, metal's body organs are the lungs and large intestines (and colon). Metal personalities must take care of their lungs, for they may be susceptible to colds, cough, flu, pneumonia, tuberculosis, and other respiratory problems. Cigarette smoking is extremely harmful for metal types. They could also develop intestinal problems that result in constipation or poor bowel function. A sunken chest or labored breathing are signs of a weak metal constitution. Lung illness and metal imbalance may result in a pale, sickly complexion.

水 Water

Water is the most feminine of the five elements and therefore is considered very yin. In Taoist cosmology, femininity is not considered weak. On the contrary, water is the most powerful element, for it can move around any obstacle in its path without losing its essential nature. Water can, in time, dissolve the hardest mountains. When water expresses masculine yang energy, its color is black, and it is symbolized by a wave. When water expresses feminine yin energy, its color is gray, and it is symbolized by a brook.

Water's planet is Mercury. The metal mercury exists in a liquid form, like water. The feng shui building or building shape of water is unique: detached houses, unusual architecture, irregular shapes, and one-of-a-kind dwellings. Buildings of the water element have a front door or entrance that is not easily visible. Water's landscape form is an irregular peak, a cupola peak, and a mountain peak with watercourses. The water room of a home is the bathroom. Water's season is winter, which corresponds to the three Taoist astrological signs of wintertime: Boar (November), Rat (December), and Ox (January). Water's direction is north, and its climate is cold. Water's symbol is a black tortoise.

Water objects in a home or office environment are all types of reflective surfaces, including mirrors, glass, and cut crystal. Water is also represented by waterways, rivers, streams, pools, fountains, and aquariums. Visual art that is abstract or asymmetrical symbolizes water, as do dark colors, including black, blue, and gray.

You may be a water personality type if your year of birth ends in the number two or three. Black years (yang water) end in the number two: 1902, 1912, 1922, 1932, 1942, 1952, 1962, 1972, 1982, 1992, 2002, 2012, 2022, and so forth. Gray years (yin water) end in the number three: 1903, 1913, 1923, 1933, 1943, 1953, 1963, 1973, 1983, 1993, 2003, 2013, 2023, and so on. (Refer to the appendix for exact dates for those born in late January or early February.) You could also be a water type if you have much of the water element in your physical constitution. This can be determined through pulse diagnosis by a doctor of traditional Chinese medicine. The home environment of a water personality type is a dark, cool room because these types are content in a basically yin environment. They require at least one room in a home to be painted in darker colors, a quiet cool place for rest. Their bathrooms can be transformed into nurturing environments for healing baths. Water types are enriched by fountains as part of the interior or exterior design. Care must be taken, since excessive water can cause melancholy.

Water character traits are creativity, wisdom, sensitivity, reflection, persuasion, effectiveness, and desire for life and sex. Water types value family and social contacts and possess the ability to attract (being receptive, water can attract rather than pursue). They are mysterious people who often internalize their feelings and think and ponder too much. The emotion fear is associated with the element water. Other water emotions are indecisiveness, vacillation, and uncertainty. Water personality types succeed by not allowing fear to block the fullest expression of creativity. The challenge for water types is to overcome their fears and become active participants in life.

In traditional Chinese medicine, water's body organs are the kidneys and the bladder. Water personalities may have a predisposition to urinary problems, bladder infections in women, or prostate difficulties in men. Coffee drinking weakens the kidneys, and cocaine and narcotics abuse causes irreversible kidney damage. All of these toxic substances, as well as alcohol, must be avoided. Kidney illness and water imbalance are indicated by dark circles or swollen bags under the eyes. Baldness is often another sign of a weak water constitution.

Colors: black (yang) and gray (yin)

Building shape: detached houses, unusual architecture, irregular shapes, and one-of-a-kind dwellings; also dwellings where the front door or entrance is not easily visible

Landscape form: irregular peak, cupola (indented peaks), and watercourses on a peak

Home environment: a dark, cool room

Room: bathroom

Taoist astrological signs: Boar, Rat, Ox

Planet: Mercury

Direction: north

Climate: cold

Season: winter

Emotions: wisdom and sensitivity when balanced, fear when imbalanced

Symbol: black tortoise

Body organs: kidneys (yin) and bladder (yang)

木 Wood

Wood is a lesser yang element. When wood expresses masculine yang energy, its color is green, and it is symbolized by a pine tree—sturdy, upright, and enduring. When wood expresses feminine yin energy, its color is blue, and it is symbolized by the flexible bamboo that bends gently with the wind.

The element wood is masculine and is considered less yang than fire. Wood's planet is Jupiter, the largest planet, symbolic of wood's growth in springtime. Wood's season is spring, the time of planting seeds, new growth, and beginnings. Its direction is east, and its climate is windy. The feng shui building shape of wood is a cylindrical structure (silo). Buildings made of wood are, of course, also considered to be of the wood element. Wood's landscape form is a mountain with a sharply rounded peak. The wood room of a home is the kitchen. Wood corresponds to the three Taoist astrological signs of springtime: Tiger (February), Hare (March), and Dragon (April). Wood's direction is east. Wood's symbol is an azure dragon.

Wood objects in a home or office environment encompass all types of furniture and accessories made of wood, rattan, and bamboo; wood paneling and siding; decks; and roofing. Fabrics, cloth, and textiles made of the natural fibers cotton, hemp, and rayon represent wood. All indoor and outdoor trees, plants, and growing things are of the element wood, including plants and flowers made of silk or plastic. Floral-patterned upholstery fabrics, linens, draperies, tapestries and other wall coverings are all considered to be of the element wood owing to the floral pattern. Visual art that depicts lush landscapes, gardens, plants, trees, and flowers symbolizes wood, as do all green and blue colors, including turquoises.

You may be a wood personality type if your birth year ends in the number four or five. Green years (yang wood) end in the number four: 1904, 1914, 1924, 1934, 1944, 1954, 1964, 1974, 1984, 1994, 2004, 2014, 2024, and so on. Blue years (yin wood) end in the number five: 1905, 1915, 1925, 1935, 1945, 1955, 1965, 1975, 1985, 1995, 2005, 2015, and so forth. (Refer to the appendix for exact dates for those born in late January or early February.) You could also be a wood type if you have much of the wood element in your physical constitution. This can be determined through pulse diagnosis by a doctor of traditional Chinese medicine. The home environment of a wood personality type is filled with lush houseplants. Wood personality types appreciate lush plants and fresh flowers because growing things attract lovely chi and exemplify the wood principle of growth and expansion. If one born in a wood year is unable to maintain live plants, fine-quality silk flowers and superior artificial plants can be used. Dried flowers are unlucky feng shui because their chi is dried up.

Wood character traits include bold actions, planning, initiating new projects, idealism, imagination, compassion, and competition. Wood types possess decision-making skills and the ability to create change. They are focused, active, driven, and competitive people. From an Asian perspective, the go-getting, do-or-die, pioneering spirit of American culture is very wood. The emotion anger is associated with the element wood. The challenge for a wood type is to learn to transform anger into kindness and channel it into positive work that benefits all people. Other wood emotions and qualities are kindness, tension, competitiveness, criticism, discouragement, regret, dislike of self and others, negative judgment, and repressed anger related to thwarted affection.

In traditional Chinese medicine, wood's body organs are the liver and gallbladder. Drinking alcohol is like drinking poison for wood personalities because alcoholic beverages heat (overstimulate) the liver and cause severe wood imbalance. Wood types must remove from their diet greasy, fatty foods that antagonize the gallbladder. Liver illness and wood imbalance are indicated as furrowed lines at the brow. (A single deep furrow between the brows indicates spleen imbalance and correlates to the element earth.)

WOOD

Colors: green (yang) and blue (yin)

Building shape: cylindrical (silo) and buildings made of wood

Landscape form: mountain with rounded peak

Home environment: filled with lush houseplants

Room: kitchen

Taoist astrological signs: Tiger (February), Hare (March), Dragon (April)

Planet: Jupiter

Direction: east

Climate: windy

Season: spring

Emotions: kindness when balanced, anger and competitiveness when imbalanced

Symbol: azure dragon

Body organs: liver (yin) and gallbladder (yang)

Taoist Alchemy: Elements in Balance

In feng shui, the balanced blend of all five elements creates a harmonious environment. This is attained by applying the nurturing, controlling, and reducing principles of the five elements.

ELEMENTS IN BALANCE

ELEMENT	NURTURES	CONTROLS	REDUCES	IS CONTROLLED BY
Fire	Earth	Metal	Wood	Water
Earth	Metal	Water	Fire	Wood
Metal	Water	Wood	Earth	Fire
Water	Wood	Fire	Metal	Earth
Wood	Fire	Earth	Water	Metal

The diagram below depicts the nurturing cycle of the elements. Fire nurtures earth because after fire burns, it becomes ash, which creates more earth crust. Earth nurtures metal because metal ores are mined from deep within the earth. Metal nurtures water because water is contained and carried in metal vessels. Water nurtures wood because watering wood (trees) helps them grow. Wood nurtures fire because adding wooden logs to a fire creates a brighter blaze.

THE NURTURING CYCLE

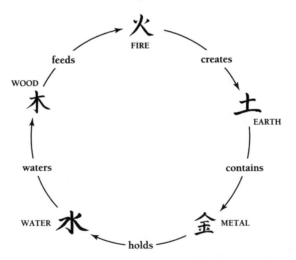

In applying the nurturing principle, take the example of metal nurturing water. If there is too much of the water element represented in a room, it is a dark, dank, depressing space. One would not want to add any water objects, such as a fish tank, indoor fountain, or dark black or blue colors to the space. Instead, add the nurturing element metal, as symbolized by the color white. Painting the walls white will brighten the room and balance the water element.

Another example is that wood nurtures fire. If plants and trees are added to a very bright, sunny, too fiery room, their greenery adds a calming and nurturing feel. Their vital chi will be uplifting and inspiring for inhabitants. Adding wood to fire is very balancing in outdoor environments through landscaping with lush vegetation.

Balance is also achieved by applying the controlling element. The diagram below depicts the controlling cycle of the elements. Fire controls metal by melting it. Metal controls wood by cutting it. Wood, in the form of trees, penetrates the earth and exerts an influence with its roots. Earth controls the flow of water by blocking it with dikes and dams. And water extinguishes fire.

THE CONTROL CYCLE

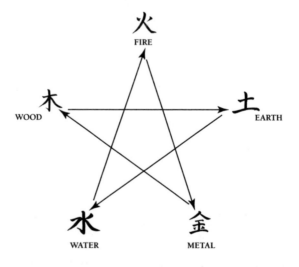

An example of the controlling cycle is that fire melts metal. Adding fire's bright colors to a stark white metal room will bring life to the space. Fire objects of interesting, colorful collectibles will melt away the alienating discomfort experienced in an overly metal environment.

The element that controls fire is water. Too much fire is exemplified in a room that is too bright. This can be found in a room with huge windows, a big skylight, or overhead fluorescent lights that emit a harsh glare. Such a yang environment can cause headaches and irritability, and creates sleeping problems in the bedroom. Simply control the presence of the fire by adding blue or black curtains, which represent the element water.

Balance is also achieved by applying the reducing element. The diagram below depicts the reducing cycle of the elements. The reducing cycle is the nurturing cycle viewed backward.

The reducing cycle works in this way: Fire burns wood, wood (trees' roots) sucks up water, water corrodes metal, metal is extracted from the earth, and earth suffocates fire. If an environment lacks an element, bring in the objects and colors associated with that element. If there is too much of an element, simply remove some of those objects and colors.

THE REDUCING CYCLE

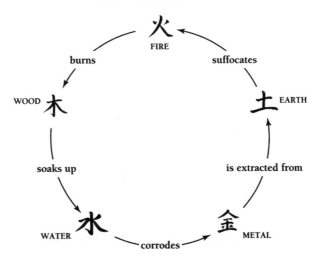

For example, an overwhelming fire room will be reduced by adding earthy colors and soft-padded furniture. Another example is that a bland metal environment can become more comfortable when the metal is reduced by adding an indoor water fountain.

In most people's homes, there is an excess of their birth year element. (Your birth year element is discussed further in chapter 8.) In these circumstances, the most practical solution is to simply remove the strong presence of that one element.

The art of feng shui is to balance all five elements in a harmonious way. In the example of too much water creating a dark and depressing room, the water element can be mitigated by adding the element wood in the form of lush houseplants or freshly cut flowers. People will feel as if they are in an exotic hothouse. Paint the walls white (metal) and add brighter light bulbs and brightly colored accents (fire), a few pieces of cozy stuffed furniture and rugs (earth), and the houseplants and flowers (wood).

A stark, all-white room represents an overabundance of the element metal. Because earth nurtures metal, the addition of a bit of earth's colors, gold or yellow, would be helpful in creating balance while maintaining the clean style. Adding green plants (wood) also balances the heavily metal environment. A water fountain or tank of beautiful fish provides focus and softens the metal. The joint effect of water and wood creates harmony—water nurtures the wood while checking the effect of metal. Another option is to add the colors red, purple, orange, or pink, which introduces the element of fire to control the metal.

Balanced interaction of the five elements brings physical harmony and good health. In traditional Chinese medicine, fire is associated with the heart. A heart attack results from too much tension (wood) and grief (metal). Both the nurturing and controlling cycles are out of balance. Fire does not receive nurturing from wood, and it has excessive control over metal. In another example, water is associated with the kidneys. Water is nurtured by metal (the lungs). The lungs are a respiratory filtering station, just as the kidneys are a fluid filtering station. And water is controlled by earth (the stomach). Water imbalance from stomach fluids and kidney fluids calcifies to create kidney stones.

SIX

....

How to Practice Feng Shui

THE ANCIENT TAOISTS were masters of intuition. They sensed the balance of chi in an environment that creates harmonious feng shui. They sensed the meridians of chi in our bodies, out of which came the science of acupunture. Through meditations on plants they came to understand the medicinal properties of herbs and created a vast natural pharmacopia. Even in modern times, people can still sense that intuitive spark that resides in the soul.

Data and research cannot tell you why you feel calm in one place and "get the creeps" in another. It simply cannot be explained in words. Instead it is known and felt. It is intuition—that little bit of human instinct, a direct wisdom that is an important part of feng shui. Our intuition knows what is good for us. Even when we logically decide what should be good for us, our intuitive sense knows the truth. Our inner wisdom connects us to nature, whereby we get a feeling for what is balanced and what is imbalanced.

To begin an assessment of the feng shui in your home or office, sit and really look at your environment. Pretend that you are a guest entering your home for the first time. What do you see? What do you smell? What do you hear? And most important, how do you feel? Some people just love their places. Others become critical. Most people's response is an appreciation for the roof over their heads, but, at the same time, a desire to change things to create a more peaceful home.

In order to apply feng shui principles to your home, you must first thoroughly clean, room by room. Clean with the mindful intention of transformation. Cleaning up and removing clutter is one of the foundations of feng shui. How can there be harmony where there is a mess? Begin at the mouth of chi as you enter your dwelling. Remove clutter from the area around your front door. That task is not easy for many people. Front porches or entryways are often heaped with potted plants, leaving only a few inches to gingerly step when approaching a home. Front steps are the resting place for more plants, or an air pump for bicycles, or recycling bins. Entryways have become the resting place for a cat litter box or an old weathered wicker chair that no one sits in. The entry light bulb burned out years ago, and no one has bothered to replace it.

Try a "mouth of chi exercise." Take *everything* away from your front area and door. Move outdoor furniture that blocks the stairs or porch. Wash clean the entryway and the front door. I recommend using a pine-scented cleaning solution and then a final rinse with saltwater. A person in rural China might use lye soap and a bucket of water and scrub with a bamboo brush, but modern westerners have many options for cleaning supplies. Find a product that is safe for the environment and start scrubbing. While cleaning, say a prayer that peaceful people and good opportunities enter through your front door.

Sense the chi in all things, and respect the vital life force in all creation. Talk to plants as though they understand you. Clip back any that are growing over the sidewalk leading to your front door. Recycle weak plants to the mulch pile. And don't keep a plant that is no longer lush and healthy simply because a tiny bud sprouts from the bottom of a cracked pot with too little soil. You must learn how to remove clutter, and dying vegetation is a good place to begin. A neglected plant can be brought back to fullness by using your intuition and sensitivity, but that is not the goal in feng shui. A lush, rich environment is desired, teeming with vital life force. When neglected, chi-deficient objects are placed together at an entryway, the feeling is neither welcoming nor inviting.

Did feng shui already lose its appeal? You want magic, not more housework? Sorry. Cleanliness is next to goddessliness, and the biggest transformation of an environment takes place when it is cleaned up. When you are done, look at the clutter-free and cleaned entryway. How does it feel? It feels five times larger! Keep looking and feeling. Rehang the mailbox if it is dangling precariously on one nail. Catch the spiders, release them elsewhere, and then sweep out all cobwebs. Are there other insects living there? They, too, must move.

Before you replace any of the old porch junk, scrutinize it carefully, as if you were a first-time guest. Has that welcome mat worn out its welcome? Once hanging plants have been taken down, it is best to leave them down. Heavy hanging objects do not feel safe, especially to a child. Droopy plants, such as spider plants, do not create good feng shui. Miraculous transformation is also accomplished by changing the lighting. In most instances, use a high-wattage bulb, at least one hundred watts. If a broken light fixture needs new glass over the bulb, fixtures can be purchased inexpensively at a hardware store.

Wind chimes liven up an area because the soft tinkling sounds are uplifting and inspiring. On a large porch, the sounds from a wind chime slow down chi that would otherwise move in a straight line right past your front door. Harmonious chi moves in a curved, graceful line, as if following the natural course of a river. Long, straight lines, such as long hallways, are better if the chi is slowed down. In a cramped entry area, the wind chime sound disperses chi that would otherwise become too heavy and dense. Metal wind chimes are preferred because wind chimes made of bamboo, wood, glass, ceramic, tile, or shell make a flat, clacking noise. When you select a wind chime, listen to its sound before you hang it. Be sure that it makes a sound that you enjoy hearing.

WIND CHIMES SLOW DOWN CHI ON A PORCH

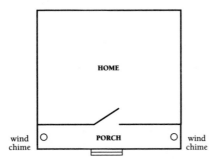

The healing is in the doing. The following tale illustrates the commitment necessary to transform the mouth of chi. For years I listened to my friend

Mary complain that she never met people, that she felt alone, and that life was passing her by. I recommended that she open the mouth of chi to her home by clearing off the front porch of her Santa Cruz, California, beach house. Mary, an earth personality type, had so cluttered her entryway with potted plants that you had to squeeze your way into her home. The screen door fell off its hinges when the rare guest opened it.

Mary removed the flowerpots from her porch steps. She also moved her out-of-season orchids to the side of her house and removed a giant cactus from the middle of the porch. Cacti do not represent good feng shui because they have spiky leaves that are not round, lush, shiny, and inviting. When entering her home, you felt as if you could be pricked by the cactus!

Mary's front door creaked so loudly when it opened that it sounded like a sound effect from a horror film. I took a bottle of vegetable oil from her kitchen cabinet and applied a few drops of oil to the door hinges. The door opened silently. It was that simple. The door was decorated with dried-flower wreaths. When Mary realized how gray, dusty, and lifeless they were, she removed them. Dried flowers are not considered to have good feng shui because they no longer contain vital life energy. If you hang herbs and plants up to dry before using them, take them down and properly store them in glass containers once they are dry. Do not leave them hanging up for months to collect dust. Chuck that dried eucalyptus that lost its scent years ago, the dusty potpourri, and the grayed baby-breath clusters. When fresh-cut flowers in a vase start to wither and their chi fades, replace them.

On the porch, Mary kept an old wooden chair with the seat falling out. That lone broken chair added to her sense of isolation. I suggested that she get rid of the chair when the neighborhood recyclers picked up discarded household items. Once it was gone, the energy of the porch changed entirely.

Change may not always be easy, but to create harmonious chi in your environment, that which is inharmonious must change. You must face your fears and *do* it. After you clean the mouth of chi to your home, a finishing feng shui touch is to place a small mirror on the front door, with the reflective side facing out. Alternatively, the mirror can be hung over your door. In this way, outside influences are reflected away from your home. This is especially effective in keeping out energy in a dangerous neighborhood. If this sounds like superstition, try it and see how you feel. I notice an immediate reduction in street noise when small mirrors are placed over a door and in windows. In a window, the mirrors can be balanced on the windowsill.

The door to a home is located in one of three guas: Heaven/helpful people, Water/career, or Mountain/knowledge. The door to Mary's beach house is in the Heaven/helpful people gua. Owing to the chaos in this area, she had felt abandoned and alone, without anyone to help her. Most front doors to a home are placed in the Water/career gua. In this instance, Mary's artist's studio is located in the Water/career gua—she is a very successful illustrator of children's books. If the mouth of chi to your home or office is positioned in Water/career, make sure that the area is clean, well lit, bright, open, and very easy to enter. This will help foster a successful career. The third option for an entryway is the Mountain/knowledge gua. That is where Mary's bedroom is situated, and she spends much time there recording and analyzing her dreams.

Regardless of which gua you enter, a key way to improve finances is to fully open and brightly light the mouth of chi to your home or office. A front door can be painted red for added good fortune. Hang a red decorative object on the front door or a door harp that makes a lovely sound whenever the door is opened. The sound will enhance good chi.

Once the mouth of chi is open from the outside, it must open on the inside. If the door cannot swing fully open in an arc, remove all the obstacles that block its movement. A clean, bright foyer is best, but if the door opens into a living room, be sure that as soon as you walk in, the entryway is not blocked by furniture. Removing obstacles is not easy for most people. In many homes and offices a desk, bureau, or table stand in the entry hall. Furniture is placed so that the entering guest must step to the side to navigate down the hallway. People adapt to twisting around furniture. When the piece of furniture is moved, they are shocked by how much space exists in a formerly small entryway.

Your front door must be able to open completely. The coat rack behind the door, the umbrella stand, the boxes for recycling paper and bottles must all be moved away. For how many years have you squeezed through your front door and banged your legs when entering your own home? Is there a coat rack full of winter coats that hang there all summer instead of being properly stored away? Are shoes strewn everywhere? Shoes belong in a closet, not in an entryway.

The diagram below illustrates the problem of an entrance hall blocked by a long, low table with family photos crammed on every inch of its surface. In this San Francisco home belonging to a single mother and her daughter, the table blocked the mouth of chi and was so low that no one could view the chaos of photos. I suggested that the photos be placed in an album. Once the table was taken away, it was as if it had never been there! The feeling changed immediately when the mouth of chi was opened. The low table was relocated onto the outdoor deck, where there was no furniture. The table was protected from rain by the deck's overhang roof. Because the table was low, the daughter placed cushions around it and created a new outdoor area for herself.

The mother and daughter were fortunate that their apartment had an ideal foyer in terms of feng shui. It led directly to their living room. This is not always the case. To enter and face a wall drastically closes a mouth of chi. In these instances, hang inspirational artwork or a beautiful piece of fabric at eye level. Do not hang a mirror on a blank wall facing the entrance. Instead of imparting a welcoming atmosphere to a place, it will usually cause your guest to start fixing her hair, fidgeting, or reapplying makeup. A mirror seen upon entering a business is especially negative and can drive away customers.

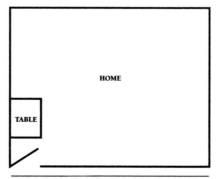

Remove furniture in the entry to open the mouth of chi.

A clean, well-lit foyer is inviting. Try replacing the forty-watt bulb in your foyer or living room with a one-hundred-watt bulb. You will be amazed how this simple change lifts the chi of your home. I cannot count how many times I walk through rooms during feng shui consultations and recommend a higher-wattage bulb. If a light fixture has outlets for two or three bulbs, use lower-wattage bulbs in each fixture. Strive for balance.

Feng shui is a vast and grand art. Ancient feng shui masters, of course, did not use light bulbs. It may seem fussy to quibble over wattage, but one must start with the small and move on to the great. This book ends with a discussion of planetary constellations that align with the ancient Chinese compass. But before we reach for the heavens, replace your burned-out light bulb, clean your porch, and open your front door.

For inspiration, here is a tale of a mouth of chi transformation. Two men lived in an ugly high-rise condominium in San Francisco but wanted to create a beautiful and peaceful space within. The man who contacted me was a student of traditional Chinese medicine who was very interested in feng shui. To gain a clearer sense of how to help him, I cast horoscope charts for both him and his partner to see why they had difficulties creating a peaceful home. The first thing that I noticed was how very compatible they were. The medical student was born in the year of the Ox, and his partner was born in the year of the Serpent. They had similar values, ideals, and goals in life. I knew that my feng shui session with them would not focus on relationship issues.

The businessman born in the Serpent year had no problems concerning his home life, but the medical student's chart indicated difficulties in this area. He had moved often during his childhood and never felt settled. At times he suffered from the conflict between his private inner world and his outer career life. I thought this man would greatly benefit from a secure and nurturing home environment where he could safely regain balance after a hectic day of medical studies.

Before I arrived at their apartment, I spent some time walking around their block to get an idea of their neighborhood. It was a nice community, with a large park across the street from their building. People were playing tennis in the park, walking dogs, and generally enjoying the lovely greenery. But when I entered their building and took the elevator to their condominium, I noticed how the people living in the building did not share a sense of community. Everyone was stuck away in their own boxes. The apartments seemed deserted.

The area outside their front door was clean, almost stark. We couldn't add any enhancements, such as wind chimes, banners, or plants, because that was against condominium rules. So I simply used a sticky gum to attach a very small circular mirror on the front door at eye level, which reflected back the very long hall and elevator doors that faced their front door. On the door-post the medical student had placed a mezuzah, a traditional Hebrew charm meant to bring blessing and good fortune.

Beyond the front door, the entryway and hall were very cluttered, full of scattered shoes and a leash for walking the dog. We moved the shoes into the bedroom closet and placed the leash in a kitchen drawer. In this way, the men developed *mindfulness* about keeping their front entry clear. The discipline of putting their shoes in the bedroom closet and keeping the leash in the kitchen drawer was worth an open hallway. Their entrance felt spacious once these tasks were completed.

The men also hung a pretty circular mirror on the side wall in the hall, to further open the space and add brightness. The mirror was not positioned to directly reflect the image of the entering guest. Instead, a guest could walk right by it and just feel the brightness. This was a nice touch. The mirror was in good condition and not smoky, cracked, or made up of many mirrored tiles.

It is best to enter into a clean foyer, entry hall, or living room. Entering a home by way of a bedroom may make you want to sleep. If you enter into a kitchen, you may overeat. If you enter into a workroom or a cluttered garage, you may overwork. Entering into a playroom encourages gambling or child-ish behavior. Entering into a dining room creates a social situation.

Be sure that the first thing seen when entering a home is uplifting and inspiring. This establishes the sensibility of a home or office and sets the tone. If you immediately see something you enjoy, you will feel content. If you see something that troubles you, you may not feel at ease the entire time you are there.

Select your art carefully. Most abstract art is chaotic and not recommend-ed as the first image. Avoid violent and negative imagery. One woman's southwestern-style home in San Diego was full of reproductions of desert images—prickly cacti and barren landscapes. This imagery was present in the entrance and was repeated in every room of the house. Her desert scenes were hung in groups at different eye levels, adding to the confusion. This did not set a calming or healing tone. She wanted to keep the southwestern theme, so I recommended that she hang reproductions of art by Georgia

O'Keeffe. Even though O'Keeffe's flower paintings and bleached skulls are abstract, their tone is soothing and spiritual. We chose the O'Keeffe art in harmony with the elements. A large red flower painting was hung on the far wall in the Fire/fame gua, which corresponds to the element fire. A large dark blue flower painting was placed on the opposite wall in the Water/career gua, which corresponds to the element water.

A feng shui colleague told me that he once entered a home and encountered a vampire poster! He recommended that the vampire be replaced with a lush landscape. I enjoy inspiring Goddess imagery and sacred Buddhist art, like a mandala. Be sure to mix imagery of both genders if you are heterosexual and seek a partner. Many women have homes full of sacred Goddess imagery, but seek male companions. In these instances, one can create balance with one-third sacred male imagery. On two occasions I consulted with single women whose emotional issue was lack of partnership. In every area of their homes were pictures of women alone. These sad and forlorn images reflected their mood. One woman placed a painting of a weeping woman standing alone on a beach and looking out to sea in her Earth/relationship gua. She replaced that image of longing with a photograph of two deer together in the woods, since her totem animal is the deer.

What is the first thing you see when you enter your home? And what is the first thing you smell? Our intuition is influenced by smell. When you enter a dwelling where the air is foul, your subconscious response is to want to leave. If the scent is sweet or inviting, you immediately want to stay. Every human and animal prefers the fragrance of roses and jasmine to the stench of pollution and smoke. This is not an intellectual process. Your reaction is an instinct, dating back to when humans lived in caves and did not eat foods that smelled rank. That is why incense and scented oils have been used in religious ritual for millions of years. If you go to church and smell frankincense, an incense made from tree resin, right away you will feel a deeper connection to God. The scent of incense in an ashram will help you attain a peaceful mental state for meditation. Realtors will bake bread or cookies in a home right before an open house. It may be a manipulative tactic, but they know how the sense of smell affects people. Even such a trivial scent as "new car" smell can engender feelings of wealth and success.

How do you respond to the smell when your front door is opened? Do you enter into a room of stale cigarette smoke? Open the windows, air out the place, and then smoke outside until you quit. Based on smell, is it obvious that animals live with you? The men in the condominium owned a dog. If I had not met their pet, I would not have known that a dog lived with them. But on many occasions, I have entered a home and smelled pet odor, especially from cats. Extra mindfulness about housekeeping is required if you own cats. Clean animal areas and empty garbage daily. Maintain a positive attitude while cleaning. Don't resent what you are doing. It is necessary to open the channels of chi. Stuck energy just stays stuck, generating the same problems over and over.

The magic of scent can transform your home or office into a very pleasant environment. Simply burn a purifying incense. These include frankincense and myrrh, sage, rosemary, copal, cedar, and sweet grass. If you do not know where to get these incenses, start with sage and rosemary, which you will likely find in your kitchen. Take some sage or rosemary and place it in an ashtray or other safe container. Crack open a window or front door, then light and fan the smoldering herbs. They will burn easily. As the herbs burn, walk through your rooms and fill them with scented smoke. Pay special attention to corners and go behind doors. If you find dirt, cobwebs, or dust balls there, get out the broom or vacuum and clean again. Think good thoughts.

Much success in transforming the chi of a home comes through the use of essential oils. Essential oils are highly concentrated essences of flowers and plants. One drop can change the aroma of a room. Most health food stores carry a selection of essential oils. Smell the different fragrances and determine which one you prefer. Trust your intuition when selecting your oils. Aroma therapy oil is dispersed into the air with an aroma therapy lamp, electric diffuser, or a scent ball that plugs into an electric outlet. The salespeople where you purchase your essential oil can help you find the best way to spread scent through your home. Aroma sprays, such as Orange Mate or Lemon Mate, are very easy to use and are portable. Avoid an air freshener made with synthetic perfumes; instead, seek the best-quality essential oils that you can find.

A good scent to start with is the all-purpose healing oil lavender. Calming scents are derived from the oils of most flowers and fruits, including chamomile, rose, orange, and grapefruit. Healing oils are clary sage, juniper, and eucalyptus. Eucalyptus is excellent for the lungs and is recommended for metal personality types. Fire personality types benefit from meditative oils, such as frankincense and myrrh and champa. Earth personality types do well with scents that uplift their spirits, such as ginger and peppermint. Cleansing oils, such as lavender, basil, and tea tree, are best for water personality types. Wood personality types do well with oils that inspire them, such as geranium and clary sage, but should avoid oils made from trees, such as pine and cedar, which may generate excessive wood.

Transform your personal living space and your office with scent. Then offer to help family, friends, and coworkers. Apply your inner wisdom to serve others. A Chinese proverb states, "If you want happiness for an hour, take a nap. If you want happiness for a day, go fishing. If you want happiness for a month, get married. If you want happiness for a year, inherit a fortune. If you want happiness for a lifetime, help others."

The mouth of chi is open, your home is clean, and the air is fragrant. Another level of cleaning is in order before you start moving the furniture. This form of cleaning is more difficult than just picking up obvious clutter in the doorway. Open your closets. Remove everything. Vacuum the closet floor and dust the shelves. Repaint the closet if it has been neglected for years. Scrutinize every item before it is replaced in the closet. Get rid of old clothes. Shoes and purses that are worn out, old towels and linens all must go. Donate what is left after a garage sale instead of dragging your unsold junk back into your home.

If you are overwhelmed by the amount of clutter in your closets, start with your drawers. Open them and remove everything. Replace only the articles that deserve to stay with you and ruthlessly throw away the rest. When in doubt, donate. Unconscious fear of never having enough makes one hoard. Stop living in fear and listen to your inner wisdom. Use your intuition. Every time you use your intuition, you reclaim your connection to nature and the cycles of growth and decay—the magic of life that our logical minds cannot understand through analysis and dissection. Your intuitive higher self knows how little you really need to live comfortably.

Carefully clean one drawer at a time, but clean it thoroughly and with mindfulness, not resentment. Recycle, sell, give away, or donate things that you are keeping for future occasions that may never arise. "I might use this blanket for a baby." Give it to the Salvation Army so that another baby can use it now. Store items that are appropriate for only one season, such as Christmas ornaments. Don't let the box of holiday trimmings sit in the living room during the rest of the year. Are your drawers full of both summer dresses and winter sweaters? Store winter clothing in a suitcase during the hot months and replace with summer clothing during the cold months.

Some of my feng shui clients have wardrobes of different sizes because their body weight fluctuates. If you are in a thin cycle, store only the best of your larger-sized clothes. If you are in a heavy cycle, store only the best of your smaller-sized clothes. When you change wardrobes, you will be delighted with the few choice garments you have saved. Buy what is fashionable if you need to purchase a few items to round out your wardrobe.

Note the words "a few items." I am amazed by how many clothes people own because shopping is a condoned addiction in our consumer culture. Many women can barely remove a blouse from the closet because their garments are packed in so snugly. One client had two dozen skirts that were so tightly crammed into a narrow closet that her skirts wrinkled each other. She spent time every morning ironing a skirt for work instead of clearing the overcrowding. I recommended that she weed out most of her skirts, store them according to season, and rehang the remaining skirts on well-made skirt hangers.

Modern feng shui application for westerners focuses on removing clutter. This was not an issue for ancient Taoists, who lived simply and did not acquire so many things. Nor is clutter an issue for most people on our planet since they do not have access to a dazzling array of consumer items. The closet packed with clothes that results in the lament "I don't have anything to wear" contains more clothes than most people in the world will own in their lifetime. So after you remove your closet clutter, don't replace it with more things that eventually bring dissatisfaction. Strive to live clutter free.

Are you a collector? Do you own fifty owl statues? Either organize them in a display case or showcase only the few best ones. One of my friends had too many seashells in his apartment. They did not appear to be sea treasures, but looked instead like a jumbled mess. His solution was to place all the shells together in one large basket, where they looked lovely.

Garages are the preeminent storage place of clutter. One client couldn't even fit her car in her garage because it was so full of old junk. It is not positive feng shui to enter and exit a littered garage every day. With the mouth of chi so choked, it is as if your life is overwhelmed with responsibilities. Remove noxious chemicals if they are stored in the garage, so that the vapors of gasoline, turpentine, and other chemicals do not seep into your home. If a washer and dryer are located in the garage, place the laundry cleaning products in a container; do not leave them strewn all over. Keep dirty clothes in a hamper. If your bed is located over an electric garage door opener, move your bed or move the electric box so the electric current does not disturb your sleep. Clean out your garage, and then clean your car. Most garages are located in the Heaven/helpful people gua. This gua also corresponds to travel opportunites. Hang travel posters of places you would like to visit. This brings your travel dreams closer to actualization as well as decorating the garage.

After your clutter is gone, walk a path through your home, as if you were simply going about your daily activities. Observe every place where you stoop to enter, bend to the side to get around a table, or open a door that bangs into a piece of furniture. Move your furniture to create a better flow of chi in your home. Here is a tale of the positive effects of moving your furniture.

I visited friends in Sonoma, California. In their home, an oversized desk blocked the mouth of chi to the living room. The desk was a Spanish-style colonial antique made of dark wood. The heavy desk was bulky and felt menacing. A sensitive person could have entered and felt that there was bad energy in the home. The desk was simply placed in the wrong location, imparting a feeling of bad energy because it obstructed the living room's chi.

My friends decided to sell the desk. They immediately hauled it into the basement to store and replaced it with a small black circular table. The chi of their home began to flow in a gentle direction. After the desk obstacle was removed, I was drawn into the spacious living room, attracted to the large picture windows that looked out onto a vineyard. Their living room seemed huge when the view of the outside vineyard became part of their home—a very different experience from squeezing into their living room while looking down to avoid banging my hip against the desk. The opening of the mouth of chi in their living room was in the Water/career gua of their home. My friends called me a few days later. Their computer software company had gone public. In this example, career opportunity entered once the mouth of chi was opened.

The most desirable spot for a large piece of furniture is in the "commanding" position. This is the position farthest away from the front door of a room, where the mouth of chi can be seen easily when one is in bed or sitting at a table or desk or on a couch. In this way, you have a commanding view of the entire room. No one can creep up on you; no activities can go on behind your back. Even if you are alone in a room and know that no one will enter, it is best to face the door. This is the position for the boss, not the employee, and for the parent, not the child.

THE COMMANDING POSITION

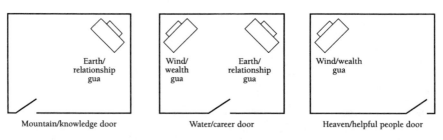

Earth/relationship gua	Wind/wealth gua Earth/relationship gua	Wind/wealth gua
Mountain/knowledge door	Water/career door	Heaven/helpful people door

The commanding position is the one farthest away from the front door.

I helped a doctor whose office desk was not in the commanding position. It was placed incorrectly on an angle in the Heaven/helpful people gua. A colorful rug matched the desk's angle. The result was a feeling of vertigo when one entered her office. We moved her desk to the commanding Fire/fame position, where she had the best view of the entire room and of

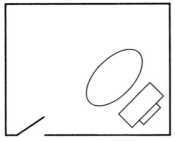

BEFORE

DOCTOR'S DESK BEFORE AND AFTER BEING MOVED TO THE COMMANDING POSITION

Incorrectly in the Heaven/helpful people gua. The angle gave a sense of vertigo upon entering.

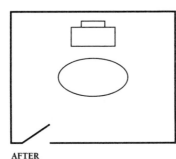

AFTER

The doctor wanted her desk to be in the Fire/fame gua because she was born in the year of the red fire Monkey. The centered rug gave a sense of order and balance.

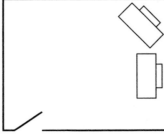

The office's Earth/relationship gua is best for commanding position.

Children/lake gua is a second option.

OTHER GOOD OPTIONS

the door. The rug was placed symmetrically in the center of the room. The room felt much larger, and the initial sense upon entering was that of order, not chaos.

Most interior and exterior spaces can be understood by applying the bagua map to each room, your lot, your building, and your neighborhood. You can balance the chi in your house room by room. Each room corresponds to one of the five elements: fire, living room; wood, kitchen; earth, dining room; water, bathroom; metal, bedroom.

Bedroom

Start in your bedroom, symbolizing the element metal. The bedroom represents the lungs of the home because metal correlates to the lungs in traditional Chinese medicine. It is here where we sleep and breathe deeply while we rest—sleep on your back or side to receive as much oxygen as possible. The bedroom is a yin room because metal is a minor yin element; a yin room is desirable for rest and peace. Your bedroom is where you nurture and take care of yourself. Remember that you spend a third of your life sleeping. Soft colors are best in the bedroom. The use of red is not recommended because it is stimulating and because fire melts metal.

Plants and flowers in the bedroom create lovely chi. Some feng shui practitioners do not recommend plant placement in the bedroom. They say that plants create too much yang vital chi which supposedly disturbs sleep. But plants give us the oxygen we need while sleeping. Plants purify the air in the bedroom while adding beauty and connecting us to the natural world. When you walk in the woods you immediately notice the refined chi of the air. This fine chi is due to the plants, so use plants in your bedroom. Plants also soften hard edges of bedroom furniture, muffle traffic noise, and offer emotional comfort. Be sure that your bedroom plants have rounded leaves, like a jade plant or rubber tree, not spiky leaves like a cactus. Flowers of good luck in the bedroom are the lily, peony, orchid, and lotus, as well as branches of flowering fruit trees such as plum, quince, orange, and peach.

People often complain that they cannot get a good night's sleep. The usual reason is that the bed is not in the commanding position. Place your bed so that the entire room can be viewed while resting your head on the pillow. But it should not directly face the mouth of chi in line with the door to the room. That would obstruct the line of energy from the door, which can disturb sleep. Nor should your feet face the door in the "coffin" position, like a corpse ready to be carried off.

Position your bed with the head against a solid wall and with equal space on either side. This creates a balanced partnership or attracts it if you are single. No bed should be set with one side against a corner wall! If the bed is

OPTIMAL BED POSITIONS

| DOOR IN MOUNTAIN/ KNOWLEDGE | DOOR IN WATER/CAREER | DOOR IN HEAVEN/ HELPFUL PEOPLE |

Where to place your bed depends on where the mouth of chi is located.

against the wall, the partner who sleeps on the outside will dominate the relationship. The only exception is made for small children—they feel more secure with their beds in this position. A parent sleeping with a small child can keep the bed against the wall to offer the child a sense of protection, but that may throw their relationship out of balance.

Do not stash boxes or shoes or other paraphernalia under your bed. Purchase a hanging shoe tree if your closet does not have room for shoes. The area under your bed must be well swept or vacuumed. If you have a bed with built-in shelves, store only items for your bed there, such as linens and blankets. Use a dust ruffle to contain the space below the bed. Solid headboards are recommended, not those made of metal bars or wooden slats. A footboard gives added security, but it should not be higher than the mattress. Canopies and bedposts may be romantic, but they are often overbearing. Antique beds may hold chi from previous owners, which can be a problem according to the principle of sympathetic magic (discussed further on page 59). Do not use them if you do not know the circumstances of the previous owners. Only use antique beds that evoke joyous memories, such as the bed where your grandmother gave birth to your mother and in which you are planning to have a home birth. Water beds, bunk beds, and magnet beds are not recommended. If you get a divorce, get a new bed. In this way, you start with fresh energy.

A large mirror in the bedroom can open the space and be used for dressing. Large mirrors on sliding closet doors can make a bedroom appear twice its size. It is just a superstition that our astral bodies rise when we sleep and become scared by their own reflection in a mirror. Use mirrors freely in the bedroom. An oval or round mirror or a fabric, tapestry, or light-weight painting is safe when properly hung over the bed, but heavy objects or hanging plants are not. Do not under any circumstances decorate the bedroom with swords or hang them over the bed. (If you must decorate with swords, mount them in a sealed glass case.)

Bed placement under a low, slanted ceiling, such as in an attic room, is not desirable. There is not enough room for chi to freely circulate while sleeping. In this circumstance, move the bed to another place. To remedy a low ceiling in a bedroom, paint it a light color. Alternatively, if the ceiling is too high, it can be painted darker colors to close the space. Ceiling beams over a bed are too heavy and can cut the space. A simple solution is to paint the beams to match the color of the ceiling.

A bedroom is a place of rest, not of stimulation with television, electronic devices, and video games. If you keep a television in your bedroom, store it in a cabinet with the doors closed. If your television is freestanding, cover the screen with a piece of fabric when it is not in use. This will impede the glare from the screen. Televisions, computers, and other electrical devices create an electromagnetic field in the environment. The unnatural chi that they emit can disturb sleep and cause insomnia, depression, and a feeling of waking up tired. More seriously, prolonged exposure to strong electromagnetic fields may be a cause of leukemia or other forms of cancers and stressed immune function. To protect yourself from electromagnetic fields, view your television from a distance of at least four feet. Replace your electric blanket with a thick wool blanket and a hot-water bottle. If your bedside stand is piled high with electrical devices, unplug them or move them to another place in your home before going to sleep. Move your bed if it shares a wall with the circuit breaker panel or fuse box in your home or if the wall on the other side of your bed is where your refrigerator is located. Move to another house if you live under a heavy power line or next to an electrical substation. Use feng shui adjustments to balance your child's bedroom if it is overly stimulating. Dramatic colors, too many toys, video games, and colorful linens depicting cartoon characters represent the fire element, which is not restful in the bedroom. Options to soften your child's bedroom are to add plants, an aquarium or indoor fountain, and gentle lighting. A child with strong fire in his or her constitution benefits from a bland bedroom.

With modern plumbing, human waste is quickly and efficiently flushed away. But before modern plumbing, a bathroom close to the bedroom was not sanitary, hence the desire to keep the bed area separate from the chi of the toilet area. Even in modern times, it is still wise to maintain a separation between where you sleep and where you eliminate waste. Therefore, if a bathroom is attached to your bedroom, keep the bathroom door closed. You do not want to view a toilet from your bed. Close the door and affix a large mirror to the outside. (An oval shape is best.) This will keep the bedroom and bathroom chi completely separate. Use a large mirror so that your head or feet are not cut off in the reflection. If you cannot hang a large mirror, at least hang a small mirror on the door at the height that reflects your face. If there is no door between the bedroom and the bathroom, install one or hang a beaded curtain or piece of fabric to create a separation between the rooms.

How does your bedroom feel? Make this room as magical and comforting as you possibly can. Use your creativity to transform your bedroom into a yin, nurturing, sacred space. Decorate with objects that have symbolic meaning for you. Use aroma therapy and scent to help you sleep well and remember your dreams. A fountain in the Wind/wealth corner of the bedroom makes the room more yin. Water is symbolic of money, and flowing water is more powerful than stagnant water. The soothing sound from a small indoor fountain can inspire a meditative and relaxing state for sleep.

The Earth/relationship gua is in the far right corner from where you enter your bedroom. It is this gua that you embellish to attract and sustain vital relationships. A pair of flowering plants, imagery of couples, objects in pairs such as crystals, and the color pink are appropriate in this corner. You might arrange objects that represent all five elements for total balance in this gua. For example, a pair of candlesticks (fire), a ceramic sculpture of a couple embracing (earth), fresh flowers or a healthy plant (wood), crystals or two metal vases (metal), and a mirror or a small fountain (water) represent all five elements.

A friend of mine could not break up with the man she was dating, even though she wanted to. I went to her home and found that a trunk full of his clothes sat directly in the relationship corner of her bedroom. We moved the trunk to the basement to store it. My friend told him that he had to take his trunk away by a certain date, or else she would get rid of the contents. He came for it that weekend. She then washed the empty corner with rosewater and placed a round table there. She decorated the tabletop with fresh flowers, pairs of shells, heart-shaped mirrors, an aroma therapy lamp with rose and jasmine oil, and east Indian art of couples in tantric embraces. She calls it her altar of love. Her difficult man is gone, and she is now engaged to a stock broker.

Living Room

The element fire corresponds to the living room. The living room is the heart of the home because fire correlates to the heart in traditional Chinese medicine. This is an exciting yang room because fire is the most yang element. The living room should be adjacent to the entryway. This is the first room a guest experiences, and for this reason it can attract new friends or repel people depending on the chi. Display your most beautiful possessions in the living room.

The living room is the main room on which to overlay the ba-gua map, and the corners and areas here reflect the important locations of Water/career, Mountain/knowledge, Thunder/family, Wind/wealth, Fire/fame, Earth/relationships, Lake/children, and Heaven/helpful people. Focus on *all* eight gua locations in the living room!

Do not neglect the Wind/wealth gua. Too often I see an empty space at the end of a living room couch in the Wind/wealth gua, with nothing there but dust on the floor. The Wind/wealth corner is located at the far left from the entry. This is a focal point for you and your family. It is best for this area to be backed by a solid wall, not windows or a doorway. If there is more than one sitting area, it is very helpful if it includes this corner. Live and flowering plants, live bamboo, beautiful silk flowers, and freshly cut flowers are excellent symbols of growth and abundance in the Wind/wealth corner. Remember that hanging plants, plants with spiky leaves, half-dead plants, and faded cut flowers do not generate good chi. Live animals enhance chi, which is why colorful caged birds or a fish tank with an odd number of fish are classic additions to the Wind/wealth corner of the living room. We are responsible for the quality of life of our animals; if you are not prepared to commit time, love, and energy to birds or fish, use an indoor fountain in the Wind/wealth gua. An indoor fountain is outstanding in terms of promoting money and prosperity. Fish tanks, fountains, and moving water have long been symbols of wealth. That is why many Chinese restaurants have fish tanks. These tanks are usually located where you enter the restaurant, in the Water/career gua.

Your living room should feel secure and well lit, especially at night. Hang curtains, roll-up shades, or fabric blinds. Slatted blinds such as aluminum Venetian blinds are not recommended, since they create shadows that look like knives. During the day open your curtains to let in the chi of the sun. Be sure to close your curtains at sunset to contain chi in your home. A direct view into your living room at night can attract thieves. If you open your curtains in the evening to view the night sky, close the curtains when you are done. Energy can be lifted in sunken living rooms or living rooms with low ceilings by placing lamps on the floor that direct light upward. Paint overhead beams to match the color of the ceiling.

A square or rectangular shape is best for a living room. If the room is of an irregular shape, a screen can be used to block off the extra space. Observe which area of the ba-gua is affected by extra space. Add enhancement that correlates to the properties of that gua, such as books in the Mountain/knowledge area. Make sure that any furniture near a doorway does not block the mouth of chi. Furniture is best arranged to face the mouth of chi. To enter a room and be confronted with the back of a couch creates confusion. It is also best to position furniture against a solid wall. You are more secure with your back to a solid wall, although guests may have their backs to windows or doorways. The head of the household is empowered by sitting in the commanding position of the living room.

Harmony with furniture is created by keeping pieces on an even line of sight. A tall and heavy yang piece overwhelms a small and delicate yin piece.

MOVE THAT COUCH!

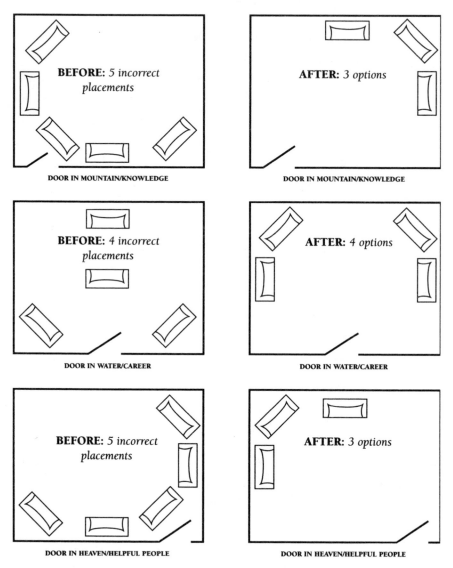

BEFORE: *5 incorrect placements*

DOOR IN MOUNTAIN/KNOWLEDGE

AFTER: *3 options*

DOOR IN MOUNTAIN/KNOWLEDGE

BEFORE: *4 incorrect placements*

DOOR IN WATER/CAREER

AFTER: *4 options*

DOOR IN WATER/CAREER

BEFORE: *5 incorrect placements*

DOOR IN HEAVEN/HELPFUL PEOPLE

AFTER: *3 options*

DOOR IN HEAVEN/HELPFUL PEOPLE

Often I see homes with too much furniture and furniture that is too heavy. This is another form of clutter. Decide which pieces to keep. Then donate the others or hold a garage sale. You do not want an overpowering piece of furniture in an important area of the ba-gua so that the gua's chi becomes stuck.

In some instances, antique furniture can hold the chi from previous owners.

This principle of transference is also referred to as "sympathetic magic." Energy connects the current owner to the previous owner. People bid wildly to own the possessions of Jacqueline Kennedy Onassis or Princess Diana. If you feel that a piece of furniture has strange energy from a previous owner, thoroughly clean it. Burn incense under the furniture to smoke it out and give the furniture time to absorb the chi of the new owners. If you are still uncomfortable every time you sit in that chair or couch, get rid of it.

A television in the living room should be stored in a closed cabinet. If the television is freestanding, cover the screen with a piece of fabric when it is not in use. Televisions are best placed away from a window to avoid glare. If it is in the Earth/relationship gua, there is a tendency to watch too much television instead of interacting with others. The characters projected on the screen become virtual companions.

A European client had an African art collection located in the Earth/relationship gua of her living room. She dated only African-American men, and her daughter was of mixed ancestry, with an African-American father. My client told me that she wanted to have relationships with many types of people, not just those of African heritage. I recommended that she put her exquisite art collection in either the Lake/children gua or the Thunder/family gua for her daughter's benefit. Then she could place imagery from all over the world, not just Africa, in her Earth/relationship gua.

The Fire/fame gua in the living room is important in terms of securing respect from others, especially to advance your station in life. My friend Donna wrote a historical novel and received a huge advance while she was living with her husband in a large apartment. Then she divorced her husband and moved to a smaller apartment. After her move, she wondered why she received so little media attention after publication of her internationally best-selling novel. The Fire/fame gua of her new studio apartment had two objects that blocked her success. An exercise bicycle and a potted palm sat next to a large picture window. The exercycle had broken, and the palm had died. Donna had the Salvation Army haul away her exercycle, and we carried the dead palm to the garbage. Her living room suddenly seemed much larger. She believed that the broken bicycle was a symbol of her writing career going nowhere and that the dead palm represented her writer's block. Donna was so inspired by the changes in this gua that she purchased a very large crystal ball and hung it in the window. Rainbows of light sparkled in her living room during the day. She joked that she lived in a disco. Within a month of removing the broken exercycle and dead palm, Donna was featured in a major magazine.

The Heaven/helpful people gua in her living room was piled with boxes of junk that she had never unpacked after her divorce. These boxes also closed the mouth of chi when one entered the living room. With my assistance, she went through the boxes and donated most of the contents, including curtains that she had never liked—a gift from her former mother-in-law, who had never liked her. The final triumph was to remove the behemoth record player cabinet that sat in her Water/career gua. This giant piece of furniture had belonged to her ex-husband, and he no longer wanted it. The record player did not work, and it was too old to repair. Once it was removed, she finally felt relieved that her marriage was over.

The chi was unblocked in three important guas. Her Fire/fame gua was illuminated with prisms of colored light, her Heaven/helpful people gua was opened up to receive, and her Water/career gua was no longer burdened with heavy furniture. The translator of the German edition of her book invited her to Europe for a series of book signings in Germany, Italy, and Malta. While in Europe, she was offered book contracts for two more novels. These opportunities arose at a time when a challenging astrological aspect of the planet Neptune opposed her sun in Cancer, which resulted in a bout of writer's block that lasted for a year. We put the feng shui improvements into play just as Neptune stopped affecting her flow of creativity. Her writer's block ended, and her European tour began.

Dining Room

Earth corresponds to the dining room—the stomach of the home, where meals are eaten. Earth correlates to the stomach in traditional Chinese medicine. This is a yin room because earth is a yin element. The yin sensibility is calm and peaceful, without distractions. The yin dining room stands in contrast to the yang living room, and the yin quality should be cultivated to keep eaters relaxed and wanting to linger after their meal. A yin environment is quiet, and for this reason the television must be turned off during meals. A round or oval dining table is more yin than a square table. Soft lighting, muted colors, gently curved furniture, and rugs or carpets add to the yin quality. The earth element relates to comfort—diners' comfort is the key concern. Candles are a perfect centerpiece on a dining room table. They add soft yin light and bring in the element fire, the nurturing element of earth. Use beeswax candles, which produce flames of purer chi. An elegant chandelier over a dining table also enhances chi. But if the chandelier is too overwhelming or hangs too low it can feel menacing, as if it is pressing down on diners. In this circumstance, hang the chandelier higher.

Excessive earth in an environment is indicated by clutter. The dining room is a room for dining, not a storage area or the place for extra kitchen utensils or a food processor or toaster. Keep the dining room clean and clear. If the dining room is attached to the living room, separate the two with overhead spotlight, a decorative screen, sensuous sculpture, a piece of furniture or bookcase, or wind chimes or a crystal ball hung from the ceiling where the rooms are separated.

For dining room seating, family members' chairs are best set against a solid wall or walls. Guests' chairs can be positioned against windows or doors. The best dining chairs have solid backs and armrests in which the diner can be comfortably nestled. The classic formation of family seating is influenced by the Confucian ethics of proper family relationships and by the Taoist balance of yin and yang. The commanding position is at the far end of the table, deepest into the dining room and facing the entrance.

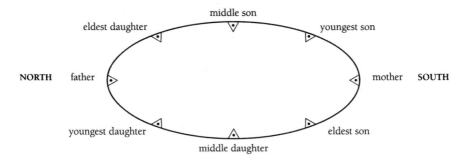

Be sure that a guest does not sit at the corner of a square or rectangular table. Eating while the corner point is directed at your stomach ruins the good earth chi you are trying to create.

You can open the mouth of chi to the dining room by removing the chair with its back to the entrance. This will open up the space of your dining room and create a pleasant flow of chi. When you enter a dining room and the first thing seen and felt is the back of a chair, the room seems smaller and uninviting. You can place the chair in an appropriate gua—such as Mountain/knowledge, where a singular chair is appropri-

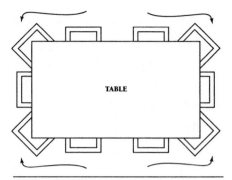

Dining chair in the wrong spot. Don't eat with a sharp angle pointed at your stomach.

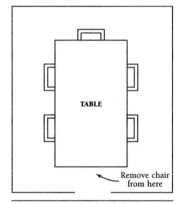

Opening the mouth of chi in dining room by removing a chair

ate—or use the chair in another room or store it in a closet until needed. Do not place the chair in the Earth/relationship gua, because a single item is not appropriate there.

Bathroom

Water is represented by the bathroom. The bathroom symbolizes the kidneys (and bladder) of the home because water correlates to the kidneys in traditional Chinese medicine. Kidneys are the fluid-filtering station of the body. The bathroom is where we cleanse, bathe, and purify. It is an extremely yin room because water is the most yin element. This one room can be small, to offer a sense of security. Keep this room as clean and free of germs as possible.

Water moves through plumbing. All plumbing must be maintained in excellent working order at all times. Water is symbolic of money; a leaking faucet indicates financial loss. Grease squeaky faucet valves and repair even the slightest plumbing problem. Don't complain about financial shortages if you won't bother to repair your leaky faucets and clogged drains.

Noxious sha chi is released from toilets and, to a lesser degree, from sink and tub drains. Close sink drains and put in stoppers when they are not in use. Always put the toilet seat down. Do not show anger or resentment when closing the lid or cleaning the toilet. Instead, express gratitude that we live with so many modern conveniences. Remember that a major concern of many people on our planet is whether their children will die of dehydration in infancy. Water is sacred. Honor it.

A small circular mirror can be attached to the ceiling over a drain to stop money from "going down the drain." Use double-stick tape and position it directly above each drain so that the mirror image reflects the drain of the toilet, shower/tub, and bathroom sink. Attach a full-length mirror to the outside of the bathroom door to make the bathroom energy "disappear" from other parts of the home. Hang this mirror in a position that does not cut off your head or feet in the reflection. The best mirror shape is oval, but a long octagon or rectangular shape will do. This mirrored door must be kept closed to be effective. Always keep the bathroom door closed. This is especially important when the bathroom is attached to a bedroom. If it is absolutely impossible to use a large mirror, at least hang a circular, oval, or eight-sided mirror at eye level on the bathroom door.

The shower and tub are best situated against a solid wall, not close to a large window. Walls and shower curtains must be kept scrubbed of all the mold and mildew that collects there. Replace towels and curtains if they become worn or stained. Most bathrooms tend to be neglected. Don't let sinks, tubs, and counters become storage areas for dozens of bottles of hair care products and cosmetics. Donate extra shampoos, conditioners, and other bath products to a homeless shelter. Toss out old cosmetics, which become contaminated by bacteria within months. Decorate your bathroom with appropriate art, such as that depicting water scenes, seascapes, or sea fantasies with mermaids or dolphins. Use the color blue. Listen to your inner wisdom in creating a bathroom that is a healing sanctuary. Experiment with many types of herbal and salt baths. A bath of Epsom salts helps release toxins from the body. Let your cares and worries go down the drain after a long, soothing soak.

Kitchen

Wood is represented by the kitchen. The kitchen is the liver of the home because wood correlates to the liver in traditional Chinese medicine. Since wood is a minor yang element, the kitchen is a minor yang room. Wood creates the fire for cooking. Healthy plants, which represent wood, add to a feeling of vitality in the kitchen.

White is the best color to paint your kitchen. Even though white symbolizes metal and metal cuts wood, white makes the kitchen look very clean. Kitchen cleanliness is most important. Repaint your kitchen when it becomes dingy. A friend's kitchen was decorated in white, black, and green, the colors of metal, water, and wood. These three colors flow in the nurturing cycle, since metal nurtures water and water nurtures wood. A nurturing color harmony is an excellent idea in any room. My friend decided to complete the entire nurturing cycle. He added the color red for fire and the color yellow for earth to have all five elements represented in harmony and balance. This color scheme created an intimate feeling in the kitchen, which otherwise was a bit stark in black and white with only the highlight of green philodendron plants.

Stove location is important because the stove, not the kitchen table, is the focus of the kitchen. Food is prepared at the stove, and food is what sustains us. The stove must be kept scrupulously clean. The ideal location for it is in the commanding position facing the mouth of chi. While preparing meals, the cook should be able to see whoever enters. If this is not possible, placing a mirror or reflective surface behind the stove allows the cook to see the reflection of those who enter. The stove should be visible from the doorway so that the cook is not hidden. A stove is best supported by a solid wall. It is not a good idea to put a stove under a window, but that would be fine placement for a sink.

The fire and water elements are imbalanced if the stove and sink are next to or directly opposite each other because the stove's fire extinguishes the sink's water. A possible solution is to hang a small metal wind chime or a crystal ball from the ceiling between these appliances to separate their energy. A refrigerator is similar to a sink in that it represents the water element, which extinguishes fire. The same solution is applicable if the stove is next to or opposite the refrigerator.

A kitchen or bathroom is not properly located in the center of the home. In this instance, mirror the walls. Even small mirrors will do. If a stove or toilet shares a wall with the head of a bed, move the bed. Care must be taken if your stove is in the Fire/fame gua in your kitchen. You may have a reputation as a wonderful cook, but there may be a tendency for accidental fires. If there are doors to the left and right of the stove or if the stove is between two doors, close the doors while cooking to prevent distractions.

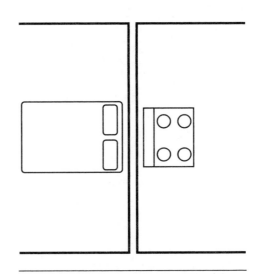

Move your bed if it is on the other side of the wall from a stove, refrigerator, or toilet.

Tiny kitchens that are positioned along a wall or set into part of a hallway to another room present challenges because chi cannot focus there. In these circumstances, use the dining room table to prepare food as if it were part of the kitchen. Another problem is a kitchen without windows. A windowless kitchen can be refreshed by a plant or painting of an outdoor scene. If a kitchen does not have a door, hang a beaded curtain, fabric, wind chime, or crystal globe centered in the doorway to separate the kitchen from the rest of the house.

A feng shui folk belief is that a mirror mounted on the wall behind the stove brings luck and money because the cooking fires are doubled in the mirror reflection. Hang a mirror behind your stove and make sure that it is low enough to reflect the burners. If you cannot hang a mirror over your stove, attach a reflective strip to the stove behind the burners. Use the stove often to maintain the nurturing dynamic between the wood and fire elements. Keep cooking utensils in good repair. Aluminum cookware can leak toxic metal into your food and should be replaced. Blunt knives can cause accidents. Microwave ovens destroy the chi in food and should be removed from your household. If you must use a microwave oven, leave the room while the oven is in use.

Consult with a doctor of traditional Chinese medicine to formulate the best diet for you. Learn to combine foods for easier digestion, such as grains with vegetables. Food can be combined, cooked, and preserved according to the five elements. The fire method of food preparation is to dry roast, the earth way is to steam, the metal way is to bake, the water way is to boil or pressure-cook, and the wood way is to sauté or fry. If you prepare your food in just one way, try variety to balance all five elements. Food can be classified as yin or yang. Yin food is fruit, and meat is yang. The balance of yin and yang in the diet will be specific to your body type, climate, season, and other factors.

Do not place the trash bin in the Earth/relationship gua of the kitchen. This is not conducive to harmonious relations. Instead, place the trash bin in the cabinet under the kitchen sink and keep all cabinet doors closed. Don't let the trash pile up. Take it out daily.

Other Rooms

For other rooms in the home, such as the office, studio, or study, a delicate balance of yang and yin is required. If clients are entertained in a home office, it is preferable for the office to be close to the front door and not set deep within the home in a power position. The power position of a home or business is the room nestled farthest away from the mouth of chi (usually occupying the Earth/relationship or Wind/wealth corner of the property). If you wish for guests to leave or for an employee to not undermine you, do not situate them in the power position of the home or office. I often visit homes where the child's room is in the power position. Care must be taken that the child isn't spoiled or indulged.

In a home office or at work, the best desk placement is in the commanding position and facing the mouth of chi. A desk receives more support if it is backed by a solid wall instead of windows, mirrors, or a corner. A desk should be well made to offer stability. A board placed over two file cabinets is not a desk. Get the best desk you can afford. A bigger desk represents more power. A round or oval desk is conducive to creative work. The chair that you sit in should be like a throne, with a high back for support. Glass see-through desktops and tabletops are not recommended.

Your desktop can be arranged like a ba-gua to focus chi while you work. Where you sit is the Water/career position. To focus chi, place a light or a candle directly across in the Fire/fame gua, add a fast-growing plant or small fountain in the Wind/wealth gua, place a photograph of you and your partner in the Earth/relationship gua, or place a family photograph in the Thunder/family gua. An editor born in the year of the green wood Dragon keeps a container of red pencils for editing located on the Fire/fame gua of his desk. The red color represents the element fire and the pencil wood symbolically feeds fire. He enjoys a very good reputation; many clients seek his skills as a Web site editor.

It is good to place the desk in the Wind/wealth corner or the Fire/fame gua. Symbols of the element water, which represents money, are desirable in an office. Water symbols include an indoor fountain and an aquarium. If your back is to the door while you sit at your desk, hang a large mirror over it to show the room's reflection while you work. Or you may place a mirror over your computer monitor to reflect what is behind you and protect your back. Mirror the walls on either side of your desk if you work in a small space. You can also mirror both sides of a tight entryway to expand it. The reflection between two mirrors is considered a great blessing.

OPTIMAL DESK PLACEMENT

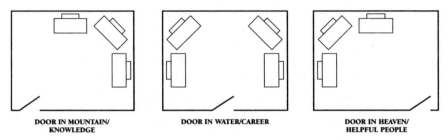

DOOR IN MOUNTAIN/
KNOWLEDGE

DOOR IN WATER/CAREER

DOOR IN HEAVEN/
HELPFUL PEOPLE

Desk placement is best in the commanding position and facing the mouth of chi, just like bed placement

The Exterior

Examine your building after each room is cleaned and transformed. Do not neglect the exterior, even though the rooms inside are cozy. Improve the condition of your home if it is in disrepair. Clean up the area around it and paint areas that need it. Maintain the general upkeep and functioning of the electrical, plumbing, and gas systems and outdoor faucets. Replace cracked or broken windows. Expand narrow pathways by trimming shrubbery. Plant vegetation to soften sharp turns around the building. Repair irregular stepping stones. Be sure that all outdoor and indoor stairs have risers.

The house's mouth of chi must be clean, well lit, and inviting. In ancient times, ceramic fu dogs symbolically guarded a main entrance and protected the front door of a building, but fu dogs clash with most modern architecture. You may prefer to use other sorts of guardians, such as small trees or bushes, to flank your building on the right and left sides if you feel the need for added protection.

The history of a building can affect the chi of the current occupants. When was your home or office built? What were the activities of previous occupants? Who died or was born there? Most important, the fate of the previous owners can influence whether the present occupants will unconsciously repeat the same pattern. It is considered lucky to move in where the previous owners had good fortune. If death or disruptive events took place in your home before you moved in, do a thorough cleansing. Paint the walls to bring in fresh chi. Wash the floors with saltwater and sprinkle salt on the floors and rugs, especially in the corners (sweep and vacuum it up the next day). Burn white candles, smoke out the rooms with incense, and play healing music in each room. Magical sounds can influence good chi and scare away negative energy. The ringing of a gong, the sound of bells, or the loud noise of firecrackers can chase out any unwanted chi. Clap your hands if you have nothing else with which to make a noise. Do this cleansing during daylight hours, not in the dark of night.

Once your building has been cleaned and attended to, the next step is to transform the lot. A square or rectangular piece of land with all four corners at ninety-degree angles is most desirable. Overlay the ba-gua map on a diagram of your lot to determine if an area of the property is missing or if another has been expanded with an addition. Obviously, the location of the main rooms, such as the bedroom, bathroom, and kitchen, may not correlate to the ba-gua map; a child's room may not be in the Lake/children gua or a bedroom in the Earth/relationship gua. Note which areas of your lot correspond to which ba-gua locations. Match your chi enhancements to the life experiences that each gua represents.

In your yard are the three important guas of Wind/wealth, Fire/fame, and Earth/relationship. Do not neglect these areas. An outdoor fountain is an excellent addition to the Wind/wealth gua because water symbolizes money. Enhance the Fire/fame area by planting red flowers, stringing lights, or painting a fence red. A lovely enrichment to the Earth/relationship gua is a garden of fragrant pink flowers to represent loving relationships. An outdoor gazebo is an excellent addition to any of the three yard guas. If the gazebo is not used often, hang a brass wind chime in the center to produce sound that will move chi even when no one is there. Colorful whirligigs are fun and a good way to move chi in a part of the yard that has yet to be landscaped.

Remember that the far-left corner of the lot from where you enter the property is where your Wind/wealth gua is located. One client had reserved this corner as a place for his dogs to relieve themselves when he didn't want to walk them. Of course, he had money problems. Another client had a garage in her Wind/wealth gua. She decided to transform the garage into a ceramics studio. During construction she yanked down the garage door.

Thousands of pecans came crashing down. Squirrels had stashed their nuts in her Wind/wealth gua. She became so prosperous that she now owns the building and tells everyone that she owes her success to the pecans in the Wind/wealth gua. She insists that the squirrels brought good fortune!

Organize the guas in your yard. Be sure that paving, walls, fences, and patios are in good repair. Keep swimming pools clean, with pumps and filters in good condition. Clean, paint, and organize garden sheds. Place lids on trash cans and recycle bins. Replace cans and bins when they are banged up and become worn.

Irregular lots can be balanced by enhancing missing guas with lights, greenery, fountains, flagpoles, gazebos, statuary, mirrors, ponds, live animals, colorful banners or flags, wind chimes, and other objects that fill in the missing space. A lot in the shape of a dustpan can suck in energy and create chaos and clutter for the inhabitants. That same shape reversed, a purse-shaped lot, is good for saving money and achieving success. A triangular-shaped lot can be balanced by adding outdoor statuary, a gazebo, or a fountain at each point. A cleaver-shaped or boot-shaped lot presents problems. It is not advisable to place a bedroom on the blade of the cleaver. Nor is it wise to place a bedroom on the heel or toe of a boot-shaped lot. An L-shaped lot is improved if the two sections can be connected in some way, usually with landscaping.

The entire Wind/wealth gua was missing from the lot of a landscape architect because the property line in her yard was cut off on a diagonal. She and her husband had aquired much debt since they moved in. To remedy the missing gua, they draped strings of little white lights from tree to tree to create sparkling energy in that area. Other solutions would be to hang kites, mobiles, or fabric from the trees to move the chi. The missing Wind/wealth gua created a projection in the Earth/relationship gua. Her marriage was very emotionally satisfying. In the Earth/relationship gua stood a little cottage where she and her husband enjoyed spending time together. The grass in the yard was dried out when she moved in. She magnified the yard chi by planting a new thick, green lawn as a gift to her husband. Her husband enjoyed the new lawn because he was born in the year of the Hare, a sign that, like a real hare, is drawn to a lush green environment.

LOT SHAPES

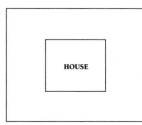

RECTANGLE

A house balanced on a lot is ideal.

DUSTPAN

Sucks in energy. Occupants tend to collect too much.

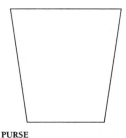

PURSE

Good for saving money and achieving success.

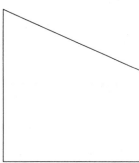

IRREGULAR

Missing the marriage relationship gua. Plant a garden with pink flowers in that spot.

TRIANGLE

Not good. Can be balanced by gazebo, statuary, fountain at each point. Still, important guas are missing.

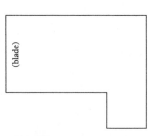

CLEAVER

Do not locate bedroom on blade. Soften the blade with outdoor greenery.

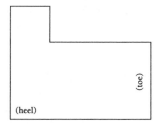

BOOT

Do not locate bedroom in toe or heel. Soften the heel and toe with outdoor greenery.

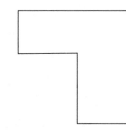

L-SHAPE

Connect the two different sections. Greenery is a creative option.

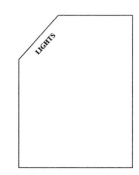

MISSING CORNER

Wind/wealth gua is missing. Try adding a string of lights.

Improve chi by planting a garden. Healthy chi is created by beautiful colors, running water, lovely scents, and an enchanting garden. Use your intuition about the plants near your home or in your garden. Plants that do not lose their foliage are preferred because they continue to hold their life chi. Yet there is beauty to the cycle of rebirth in spring of plants that lose their leaves in winter. Are roses nature's scented beauty or a thorny problem? In a rough urban neighborhood, the thorns are protective against intruders. Enter and be pricked. But in a gentler area, thorny plants are not advisable, especially close to the front door.

Learn about the types of trees, plants, vegetables, and flowers that grow well in your climate and soil and the amount of sunlight they will need. A mirror at the end of your garden will open it up and make it appear larger. A feng shui garden is based on the Taoist concept of yin and yang: dark and light areas, straight and meandering pathways (that lead to magical places), stationary rocks next to running water, and a balance between sun and shade. Create natural areas that lead to private spots for rest and contemplation. The feng shui garden is not a symmetrical well-manicured English garden. Instead, plants need little tending and grow naturally, as in a bamboo grove. Little pathways are ideally set in curved lines to gently move the chi. Ponds, especially those stocked with fish, represent increased wealth. It is a good idea to design ponds that are asymmetrical, to symbolize the element water. Pond banks should slope gently and be planted with lovely flowers, such as the water lily. The Chinese bred goldfish from red carp. The Japanese further developed the art of carp breeding to create the beautiful coi fish available to modern gardeners, landscapers, and horticulturists. As lovely as the Japanese bonsai tree may be, it is not recommended in feng shui owing to its stunted growth—especially not in the Wind/wealth gua of a room or garden.

You can overlay the ba-gua map on your garden or match the garden areas according to the five elements. Fire is represented by lighting; cooking areas, such as a barbecue; pet and other animal areas; statuary of animals; and pointed shapes. Earth is symbolized by rock gardens, ceramic pots, bricks, tiles, and square or rectangular shapes. Metal is epitomized by metal garden furniture and sculptures, chimes, sand, and oval or arched shapes. Water is embodied in fountains, reflective surfaces, mirrors, and free-form, irregular shapes. Wood is represented by wooden furniture, such as rattan and wicker; all plant material; floral and striped patterns; and long columnar shapes.

Create a garden that appeals to all five senses: to see objects of beauty; smell fragrant flowers and grasses; taste edible herbs, fruits, and flowers; hear wind chimes or bells; and touch or place your bare feet on soft mosses. Invite nature into your garden with bird feeders and birdbaths (but not if cats are near). Plant flowers that attract butterflies and hummingbirds.

A feng shui colleague, Kathy, greatly enhanced the Thunder/ family gua of her house. This gua in her home was also located in the Thunder/family gua of her lot. There was a problem with her husband's adult daughter from his first marriage. The daughter had been twelve years old when her parents divorced. As the eldest child, the daughter identified with her mother and rejected her father. The other four children had a loving relationship with their father, but the eldest daughter had not spoken to him for sixteen years. Kathy felt the family pain, even though the problem did not involve her directly. Being born in the year of the Tiger, Kathy had to pursue her goal, and nothing could stop her.

The Thunder/family gua of Kathy's home was a small area off the living room that was designed to be a dining room. Instead, it was used as a music room because it was so small. The room furnishings were a piano, love seat, and hassock. The first thing Kathy did was to create, frame, and hang collages of family photographs on the music room walls. She used pictures of all the children growing up, including the eldest daughter. Her stepdaughter's siblings had recent pictures that included the estranged daughter. These pictures were framed and hung as if the daughter had never left the family. Kathy bought a picture mat with five cutouts to feature the baby photos of all five children. A recent portrait of the daughter was placed on the piano. Next to the framed portrait Kathy set a red ribbon inscribed with the words "There is healing." Red is an auspicious color and very good to use in feng shui. A rock anchored the corner of the ribbon to add stability. Kathy also placed a poem about love next to the ribbon and rock. The ribbon, rock, and poem were positioned under a lamp so that they were illuminated every time the lamp was turned on. When she turned on the lamp, Kathy said a silent prayer and held in her mind's eye the picture of her stepdaughter's return.

Kathy added a fish tank to the room to enhance chi and keep it moving when the room was unoccupied. As go people, so goes chi, and days could pass without anyone entering this area of the home. She learned the art of keeping an aquarium and created an exquisite saltwater marine tank to which she added nine exotic fish.

There was no door between the music room and the living room. This is considered an "empty door," and it is best to separate the rooms with a crystal ball, wind chime, or fabric or beaded curtain. To demarcate the rooms, Kathy hung a wrought-iron heart-shaped chime from India with five large metal bells that represented her five stepchildren and three smaller bells that represented her three grandchildren.

A large picture window looked out onto a lawn with shrubs. Kathy removed the shrubs and planted five blooming gardenia bushes and three pink bougainvillea vines, again to represent the five children and three grandchildren. She installed a small fountain to activate chi with the running water. She then

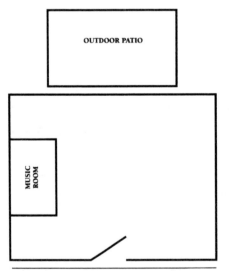

placed an oak and metal park bench that seats four and a ceramic mother goose with one gosling chick under the bougainvillea. She added a bird feeder and was mindful to keep it full of seeds. Every day it was mobbed with wild finches and songbirds.

A large patio was situated in the Fire/fame area of the yard. Kathy added stepping stones from the area she had created to attach it to the large patio, the

Front door in Water/career gua. The music room is located in the Thunder/family gua of the home and of the lot. The patio is in the Fire/fame gua of the lot.

place of family celebrations and gatherings, as if to bring the daughter back to the main family. The entire time she visualized the best possible outcome and prayed for the daughter's return. She completed this summer project in October. In November the daughter called her father and said, "I have no excuses. I just want to heal and join the family." When the daughter returned to her father's house, she saw her pictures in the music room, including her portrait. She felt at ease, and her adjustment back into the family went very smoothly. Kathy's feng shui efforts worked because she mindfully embellished the Thunder/family gua to the best of her ability.

The lot of your business requires the same attention to cleanliness as your home. It is wise to create harmony and unite the neighboring businesses that share the lot with you. It is best if commercial buildings have the same height and are unified in design. Harmony is achieved with matching awnings, facades, roofs, colonnades, and similar lighting and colors. Storefronts should not be in a straight line corridor because chi moves by too quickly. Slight variations in the depth of storefronts, with some extending out and some recessed, create a better balance. The position of the front entrance must be easy to find if the business is to be successful. The address should be clearly visible. Use large, prominent numbers and letters. Multiple entrances can be confusing and can dissipate chi. It is usually best to focus on one main entrance.

Customers feel most at ease where there is a combination of yin and yang space. Introduce the yin element of restful, open, and semi-open spaces among the yang storefronts and offices. The balance of yin and yang can be achieved with landscaped courtyards. Lush plants foster good chi and abundant wealth. Fruit trees impart beauty. Pines and other evergreen fir trees add strength and specifically represent the element wood, symbolic of growth. Willow and bamboo may be used, since they stand for grace, pliability, and rapid growth. The addition of an internal courtyard with a fishpond or fountain will help money flow for all businesses.

Once you have attended to your lot, observe the road in front of your building and how it influences the inhabitants. Most suburban homes and businesses are set back from the road with nothing to demarcate the road, lawn, and building. Plant shrubbery on the outer side of the lot or build a wall to separate the road from the property line. Even a few large shrubs or trees will have a positive effect in blocking the road's straight line of chi as it races past your front door. Be sure not to plant a tree or shrub directly in front of the entrance to your building because it will block the mouth of chi. Auspicious trees for the front yard do not lose their leaves in winter. All evergreens, especially the yew pine, impart positive feng shui. Pine, cypress, and willow are symbols of longevity. Brick walls are acceptable, but build them with gently rounded corners, not sharp angles. The wall should be in proportion to the building and not too high. Match the wall's height to the windowsill on the ground floor. If the back of your lot ends at a road, add a fence or shrubbery to contain the chi of your building. A neighboring building that is taller than yours can dwarf your home. One possible solution is to plant fast-growing trees that do not lose their leaves in winter.

It is an unforunate circumstance to have your building situated right at the end of a T-intersection. Chi enters your building too directly and powerfully. Affix a mirror or reflective brass knocker to the front door to reflect away the strong energy from the street. Adding an outdoor fountain in the front yard is ideal. A cul-de-sac or dead-end street can catch and hold too much chi and cause confusion for residents. Affix a mirror over your front door. In this way, the excessive chi is reflected away. Install a fountain, outdoor sculpture, or flagpole in the cul-de-sac to disperse the energy.

If your building is at the top or bottom of a hill or if a bridge directly faces your property, deflect chi by hanging a mirror on your building. This mirror can be placed on a fence at eye level, over a door or window, or in a window with the mirror's reflective side facing outward. Where the bridge ends and your property begins, install a fountain, flagpole, or sculpture or plant trees or shrubs to create a separation. A building situated at the curve of a road benefits from a mirror so that the road is reflected away. Planting shrubs also helps block the road's chi.

Buildings situated on corners may be robbed more frequently. Place mirrors in every window to guard in all directions. Guard dogs and a security alarm system quickly boost protective chi because they add the element fire. Busy traffic can be slowed down with a large brass chime hanging in front of a building. These simple measures help protect inhabitants and decrease traf-

BUILDINGS AND ROADS

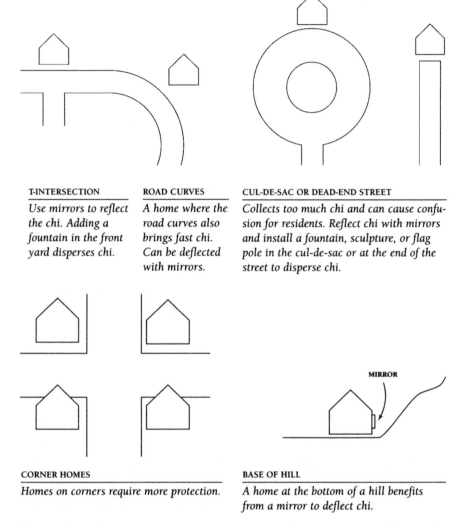

T-INTERSECTION

Use mirrors to reflect the chi. Adding a fountain in the front yard disperses chi.

ROAD CURVES

A home where the road curves also brings fast chi. Can be deflected with mirrors.

CUL-DE-SAC OR DEAD-END STREET

Collects too much chi and can cause confusion for residents. Reflect chi with mirrors and install a fountain, sculpture, or flag pole in the cul-de-sac or at the end of the street to disperse chi.

CORNER HOMES

Homes on corners require more protection.

BASE OF HILL

A home at the bottom of a hill benefits from a mirror to deflect chi.

fic sounds in their environment. Pets are especially sensitive to traffic sounds because animals are more yin than humans—animals are attracted to the most yin spot in a room or building, while we humans usually benefit from a bit more yang energy. When a truck passes your building, you may not even feel it, but an animal will.

The chi of your neighborhood is important for you and your neighbors' development and well-being. Peaceful relations between neighbors creates general harmony for all inhabitants. Observe the type of neighborhood that you live in. Obviously, living in a wealthy neighborhood creates opportunities for wealth. Living in a run-down area that lacks vital chi can deplete your strength. The types of animals in your neighborhood are a good indication of the types of chi. Wildlife indicates abundant chi.

Live on terra firma—solid land! A neighborhood built on landfill cannot offer stability to those who live there. It is not advisable to live on landfill, on floodplains, or on land that was once a toxic dump or burial ground. It is also not wise to live at or below sea level. Fortunes rise and fall like waves for inhabitants of a neighborhood located by the sea.

Observe the shapes of lots and buildings. Building shapes correlate to one of the five elements. I am fortunate that my San Francisco neighborhood represents all five elements. Most buildings are classic Victorian, earth-shaped rectangular buildings with flat roofs, on rectangular lots. There are a few A-frame (fire-shaped) homes interspersed on the block. Two domed buildings of the element metal are the Integral Yoga Institute ashram across the street and the landmark Dolores Mission church, with original Spanish-colonial mosaic domes. Architecturally unusual buildings are found on a few lots (representing the water element), and a river used to run next to the mission church. Wood is not lacking, since most of the buildings are made of wood, and in the middle of the street are miles of lush green islands with huge Canary Island palm trees that are home to a flock of wild parrots. The vast Dolores Park is a gathering place for residents that binds together the entire community.

Too much of an element can cause an imbalance in a neighborhood. For example, sections of Oakland and Berkeley, California, suffered from excessive wood. Almost all the buildings were constructed of wood, and the land was thick with overgrown eucalyptus trees that grew more quickly and dried out the native foliage. According to the nuturing cycle of the five elements, wood creates fire; and indeed, a violent fire burned down this neighborhood.

....

SEVEN

Feng Shui Solutions

SOME PRINCIPLES OF FENG SHUI may not apply to the conditions of modern Western culture. For example, trees are best on the northwest side of a house in China to protect occupants from the yellow dust blown in from the Mongolian border. Mongolian dust is probably not a problem where you live. Warm, soft winds from the southeast are lovely in China, and it is favorable for a Chinese house to face that direction.

Most modern city dwellers may have little choice concerning which direction their homes face and are relieved to find any affordable housing. Many feng shui principles can help create harmony and beauty in the modern world of concrete jungles and sprawling suburbs. Massive remodeling of structures is not required. Instead, balance of yin and yang, knowledge of the five elements, mindfulness in maintaining cleanliness, and sincere application of feng shui solutions—some as simple as rearranging a piece of furniture—can start you on your journey to peace.

One tool used to create feng shui solutions is a mirror. This light-refracting object expands an area and brings light into enclosed spaces. Use high-quality mirrors that are not warped and are securely set in solid frames. Mirrors must be clear and clean—not smoked, etched, cracked, chipped, or made up of many mirrored tiles. A beveled mirror can be used if the bevel is a border decoration. Hang mirrors at eye level, and be sure your head or feet are not cut off in the reflection of full-length mirrors.

Mirrors are an excellent addition to many ba-gua areas as a method to enhance chi and bring in light. They are especially effective in the Earth/relationship and the Heaven/helpful people guas. A mirror is not recommended for the Wind/wealth gua. A mirror's light may attract money, but it can also reflect money away, making it easy to overspend and difficult to save. Nor should a mirror be placed in the Fire/fame gua because the mirror is a symbol of water, and water extinguishes fire. As discussed earlier, it is also not a good idea to hang a mirror where it will be the first thing seen when entering a home or office.

Mirrors can be used to repel external energy. A mirror can be placed over a front door to deflect traffic noise or over the back door to deflect neighborhood activity. Circular convex and concave mirrors work well for this purpose because they encompass a large area in their reflection. A convex mirror will expand an image and is best used indoors to expand a gua's chi. A concave mirror is better used outdoors because it reverses the reflected image and thereby diminishes its influence.

A mirror can also reflect an area back into a home. For example, if a child's room is located away from the main area of a home, position a mirror immediately across from the entrance to the room. This will probably be in the Fire/fame gua. Whoever enters the room will be reflected back to join the rest of the household. This is especially useful for a teen who feels alienated from the family.

A large mirror should be hung over a fireplace in your home or office to control the fire (water extinguishes fire). It is fine to burn candles on the ledge over the fireplace, since the original purpose of the fireplace was to create fire. But do not place pictures of living family and loved ones on the ledge, only photos of the deceased. Fire tends to create earth, and an earth environment is cluttered. Don't let the area around your fireplace become cluttered.

It is best for a bed to be in the commanding position of the bedroom, with a view of the mouth of chi. But the commanding position may not always be available. When I lived in Sausalito, California, my bed could not be in this position because a closet took up half of that wall. A window was set in the other wall that faced the mouth of chi, making it too cold and drafty. Of the other possible locations, one was blocking the direct line of chi, another was in the coffin position, and a third was next to the door. I chose to set the bed next to the door, with a large mirror on the opposite wall to reflect the mouth of chi toward the bed. This mirror opened up the room, and I used it as a dressing mirror.

UNDESIRABLE BED LOCATION WITH MIRROR SOLUTION

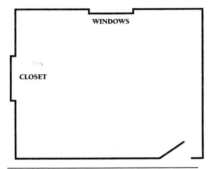

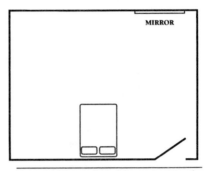

Closet in Thunder/family gua and windows in Fire/fame gua make two best spots unavailable. The Wind/wealth gua is not good for a bed because the bed is too close to a wall and not evenly spaced.

Door in Heaven/helpful people. Mouth of chi seen in mirror reflection.

A feng shui mirror in an eight-trigram frame can be purchased in Asian markets and through feng shui supply houses. The trigram arrangement on these mirrors differs from that of the ba-gua map. Students are always puzzled as to why the ba-gua map applied to rooms, buildings, and lots is not pictured on these mirrors. It is because the trigrams on the mirror frames depict an earlier form of the ba-gua.

The earlier ba-gua, known as the early heaven sequence, was created by the Taoist sage Fu Xi. Fu Xi paired the eight trigrams according to their opposites. Heaven is paired with Earth, Fire with Water, Mountain with Lake, and Wind with Thunder. Fu Xi observed how these pairs act upon each other in the natural world. He arranged the trigrams in this early heaven sequence with the opposites across from each other. Moving clockwise from the top, Heaven opposes Earth, Wind opposes Thunder, Water opposes Fire, and Mountain opposes Lake.

FU XI'S EARLY HEAVEN SEQUENCE

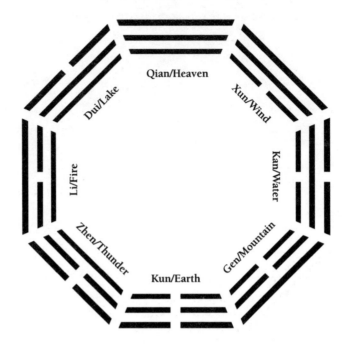

During the Zhou dynasty, King Wen rearranged the trigram sequence to represent interactive cycles according to his philosophy of the unity of heaven and humanity (whereas Fu Xi's trigrams express the interaction of natural forces without the involvement of humanity). His creation is known as the later heaven sequence. It is this arrangement that is used today in the art and science of feng shui. King Wen's "later heaven" ba-gua is made up of the eight trigrams in the sequence and shape shown in the diagram on page 83.

Another light-refracting object that helps adjust chi is a crystal ball. For modern feng shui purposes, the type of crystal used is not a crystal mined from the earth. Instead, it is a leaded glass crystal ball cut to be multifaceted and to reflect light from all directions. Long chandelier-type crystals and those that are not round are not recommended because they have no balanced shape. A forty-millimeter faceted crystal ball is the type commonly used for most feng shui solutions. I prefer a sixty-millimeter ball because it is so beautiful and powerful. A

KING WEN'S LATER HEAVEN SEQUENCE

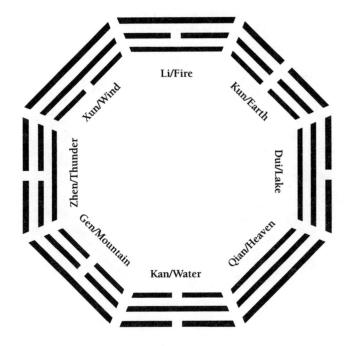

millimeter size-conversion chart for faceted crystal balls can be found on page 84.

A crystal ball adjusts the direction of chi and can substitute for a mirror. It can be placed on a desk or tabletop in any gua to add light and beauty. Many feng shui solutions call for a crystal ball to be hung on a nine-inch red ribbon. (Or a multiple of nine inches: nine is considered a powerful number because it is the highest and most yang of the single digits. Red symbolizes life, vitality, and abundant chi.) It is best hung in a window—the light refracted through a crystal ball is a perfect enhancement for all guas and creates protection and spiritual blessing. It also brings peace while sleeping in a bed located under a window, because the crystal ball's refraction of light breaks up the chi coming though the window.

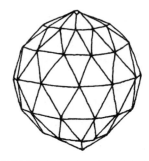

Crystal balls are hung on nine inches of red ribbon, or a multiple of nine inches.

The ten-millimeter crystal ball is three-quarters of an inch in
  diameter. These tiny ones are too small to be of much use as
  feng shui corrections.

A thirty-millimeter crystal ball is one and one-quarter inches in
  diameter. This size is often used in a car, hung from the
  rearview mirror on a red cord.

A forty-millimeter crystal ball is one and three-quarters inches
  in diameter. This is the standard size and is often used in
  stairways and hallways.

A sixty-millimeter crystal ball is two and one-half inches in size.
  This size is extremely useful for all problems and is especially
  effective when hung from windows and in the Fire/fame gua.

A seventy-millimeter crystal ball is three inches in diameter.
  This size is used for large stairways.

Sha (negative) chi collects in long, straight halls. The long hallways in
hotels and condominiums rarely feel inviting. Create harmony in long halls
by slowing down the chi. Hang crystal balls from the ceiling at intervals
throughout the hallway; most have overhead lights that will reflect through
the crystals. Other embellishments to slow chi are metal wind chimes, furniture separating long stretches of space, evenly arranged potted plants, a pat-
terned carpet and decorative curtains, and art hung at eye level that depicts
peaceful imagery. Use an aroma therapy spray or essential oil diffuser if odors
collect in a hallway.

The chi of misaligned doors can be balanced by hanging a crystal ball
between them, from the ceiling. Misaligned doors that open to face a wall can
benefit from both a crystal ball and mirrors. Hang a crystal ball where three
doors come together or where doors meet at a forty-five-degree angle. Sliding
glass doors do not feel secure. Hang a crystal inside from the ceiling to catch
the reflection of light as it enters through the glass door. On the outside, hang
a wind chime. Sliding glass doors should fit well into their frames, slide eas-

ily and not wobble, and have no gap between them when closed. Half doors, also known as Dutch doors, are also not secure and are best kept closed.

SOLUTIONS FOR MISALIGNED DOORS

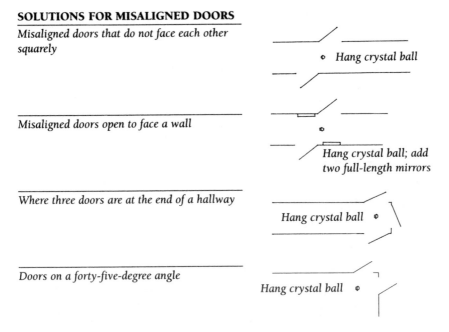

Misaligned doors that do not face each other squarely

Hang crystal ball

Misaligned doors open to face a wall

Hang crystal ball; add two full-length mirrors

Where three doors are at the end of a hallway

Hang crystal ball

Doors on a forty-five-degree angle

Hang crystal ball

It is most desirable for a door to open *into* a building, to allow chi to enter. For most businesses, however, fire regulations dictate that doors open outward. One solution is to hang a crystal ball from a nine-inch red ribbon from the ceiling, to contain chi every time the door opens. If a door is "dead," meaning that it is not opened or is rarely opened (such as a door to a storage room), affix a round or octagonal mirror on the door at eye level so that the chi around it does not stagnate.

Doors that open directly onto a stairway cause chi to quickly leave the building every time the door is opened. Inhabitants may not keep money, work may not bring about the desired results, and it may be difficult to maintain good health. In this circumstance, hang a crystal ball or wind chime from the ceiling between the door and the staircase, to slow down the movement of chi. If a door opens to a stairway that leads down, chi becomes stuck at the base of the stairs, making it difficult to achieve success in the world. It is wise to hang a crystal ball or wind chime from the ceiling between the door and the stairway in this instance as well.

Two staircases positioned next to each other, one going up and one going down (like escalators), create problems, especially if a front door opens onto them. Hang a sixty- or seventy-millimeter crystal ball from the ceiling between the two staircases, accompanied by art that depicts symbols of harmony on the surrounding walls. Art on the wall of a long, steep stairway helps climbers move up the stairs more easily and draws chi up the staircase, especially if the art shows upward movement, for example, cranes taking flight, trees that point skyward, or flowers reaching for the sun.

The downward movement of a spiral staircase drags chi down with it. Hang a sixty- or seventy-millimeter crystal from the ceiling at the top of a spiral staircase. A large plant at the foot of the stairway has an uplifting effect. You can also wrap silk vines around the stairway to suggest upward growth. Wrap vines around posts and columns in large rooms and warehouses to soften their heavy feel.

A healer I knew lived in a Victorian apartment in San Francisco. Her front door opened onto a very long and dark stairway. The top of the stairway turned at a ninety-degree angle, whereupon a few more stairs led up to a landing surrounded by five doors! A forty-millimeter crystal ball was hung from the ceiling at the bottom of the stairway. The light fixture was repaired, the walls painted, and the carpet cleaned. A wind chime was positioned at the top of the stairs at the ninety-degree angle, to help move the chi up the last few steps. Three photographs of blossoming lilies were hung on the walls, evenly spaced, to impart a sense of upward progress.

Solutions were applied to all five doors, which led to the bathroom, bedroom, office, kitchen, and living room. A large oval mirror was affixed to the bathroom door. The door to the bedroom was kept closed, and a red tassel was hung from the doorknob to add focus. Purple fabric panels, the color of wealth and royalty, were used as a door to the office, which was where the Wind/wealth gua was located. The doors to the living room and kitchen were "empty," and for this reason two pretty beaded curtains were draped in the door frames. The kitchen beads were left down, and the living room beads were pulled open and hooked at the sides to the frame. In the middle of the foyer a delicate Balinese mobile was suspended from the ceiling. Implementing these simple solutions imparted an immediate feeling of peace and harmony.

A crystal ball can be hung from a slanted ceiling to move trapped chi. Place the crystal ball a few inches down from where the ceiling starts to slope. This is especially important if a bed is placed under a slanting ceiling, as in attics; it will aid restful sleep. Hang a large crystal ball in the middle of any ceiling that is not at least six feet in height, to disperse chi and open the space. If one wall is shorter than the others, mirror it to further open the space. The mirror must be in one large piece, not put together from many tiled surfaces.

CRYSTAL BALL SOLUTION FOR A SLANTED CEILING

Hang crystal ball to slow chi

Mirror the shorter wall to expand it. Use a solid large mirror, not many mirrored tiles.

The movement of cars can disturb sleep. If your bedroom sits over your garage, hang a crystal ball over each car. If you use an overhead fan in your bedroom, you can soften the sensation of being cut by its blades by dangling a crystal from it. Although fans are not recommended, if they must be used, hang them as high as possible and add a crystal ball. A crystal ball can also be hung over any spot where you need to focus your attention: from the ceiling over the desk where you work if you are scattered, forgetful, or unable to gather your thoughts, over the dining room table so that the family eats together and savors the meal, or over the place where the cook stands in the kitchen to concentrate energy while preparing food.

There are many uses for a forty-millimeter crystal ball on a nine-inch red ribbon. Hang it in windows to add rainbow light to a room (especially in a western-facing window, to reduce glare); in the center of a small, closet-like room to expand the space; in the door frame of a room without a door; at the end of a hallway; or over a bed to stimulate a relationship.

Mirrors and crystal balls are very helpful tools to move and enhance chi, but there are many other ways to foster the same effect. The sound of wind

CRYSTAL BALL SOLUTIONS FOR INCORRECT BED PLACEMENT

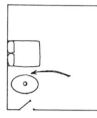 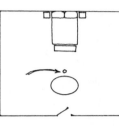

Slow down the chi that enters and directly hits the bed by placing a rug on the floor and hanging a crystal ball from the ceiling between the door and the bed.	This bed is in the coffin position, feet to the door. Slow the chi that enters with a rug, hang a crystal ball between the door and the bed, and add a chest with objects on it at the foot of the bed to block the chi. The chest should not be higher than the bed.	The crystal balls hung in the window disperse the chi entering the bedroom and directly facing the bed. Mirror corrects bed placement.

chimes, bells, healing music, and sacred chants is helpful. Play spiritual music in a room for a few days to transform the energy. Hang a wind chime in halls or interior spaces with sharp turns, to help the chi circulate. A wind chime can even be hung inside a closet if it is located in an important gua, such as the Earth/relationship corner. Don't forget to ring it occasionally. Hang the wind chime from a nine-inch red ribbon, the same as you would a crystal ball. If an entryway is very low, such as the doorway to a garden apartment, hang a bell in the door frame to lift the energy. An Irish harp or bells affixed to a low door are an extra embellishment, since the pretty sound lifts chi whenever the door is opened and closed. Bunk beds do not have a positive effect on the person who sleeps in the bottom bunk. If you must have bunk beds, hang a bell from the bottom of the top bed to lift the chi, and ring the bell often.

Living things always add life to a room. Healthy, lush houseplants with round leaves and high-quality silk plants impart a sense of vitality. The addition of three or nine healthy potted plants with round leaves brings harmony to the home or office. Flowers are especially effective in a reception area. Freshly cut flowers create wonderful chi, but they must be replaced or discarded as soon as they start to wither. Plants are an ideal solution to hide a sharp or jutting angle that protrudes into a room. If the sharp corner of a piece of furniture seems like an arrow pointed at you while you sleep, eat, or relax, position a plant in front of it. A green plant in a red pot is recommended for the back of the toilet in the bathroom. A silk plant can be substituted if the bathroom does not receive much light. Use artificial plants that look most like live plants and put real dirt in their pots.

Creatively landscaped green areas impart life and vitality to any property. Strive for variety in your landscape and replace dying vegetation and trees if they do not thrive in your climate and soil. Use plants that grow naturally in your area. Outdoor vegetation, such as a hedge, can separate your building from difficult neighbors. If land slopes sharply, plant a hedge to avoid erosion. Bamboo is an excellent addition to the Wind/wealth corner of your yard. It grows quickly and symbolizes positive life development because each branch becomes longer as it grows.

Healthy and tame pets invite good chi. Lively animals are a blessing and deeply enrich the quality of our lives. Sick or mean pets create sha chi. It is your responsibility to retrain a cat that claws children or a dog that barks at night. Fishbowls and aquariums also invoke positive chi; but you must keep fishbowls and tanks clean. Immediately replace a fish if it dies. Don't let a belly-up floater ruin the chi for the other fish! The ideal number of fish is nine—eight red and one black—or a multiple of nine in a larger tank. Nine is a lucky and powerful number, the highest of the single digits, and the color red adds life and vibrancy. The one black fish absorbs any negative chi in your environment because the color black absorbs light. Start with three little goldfish in a bowl and graduate to a five-gallon tank once you are sure that you are capable of maintaining pet fish. Do not purchase a large fancy aquarium with the intention of increasing your wealth and then neglect your fish. These sensitive and delicate creatures need care and dedication. Decorate your fish tank with golden coins, jewelry, semiprecious gemstones, colored glass, and symbols of wealth, as if you've discovered a pirate's treasure.

Heavy objects, such as stone or porcelain sculptures, smooth and beautiful rocks, large natural crystals, and other sculptural pieces, are useful to add emphasis or to ground the energy in a gua. Do not use any heavy object or sculpture that is ugly or jagged or causes a chaotic or upsetting emotional reaction. Sculptural objects, such as statuary of Saint Francis, the Buddha, or Kwan Yin (the Chinese goddess of compassion), are recommended as focal points for a garden. Heavy articles placed in a room over a garage help ground the energy. They may also be useful in penthouses or rooms with skylights, where there is a floating feeling, a sensation of not being connected to the earth. If you have just started a new job, place a heavy stone in the Water/career gua or the Fire/fame gua to secure your new position. Set a heavy stone in the Earth/relationship gua to stabilize an unstable relationship, but remove the stone after a time so as not to create stagnation or blockage.

The movement created by mobiles, flags, windmills, and whirligigs circulates chi. It is best if mobiles are hung on nine inches of red cord or ribbon (or a multiple of nine inches). Mobiles settle chaotic chi and, when placed in a corner, can liven up stagnant chi. Moving objects are fun in children's rooms. Outdoors, where they can catch the wind, they add color and a sense of whimsy. A windmill or a flag works well to break up chi collected in a cul-de-sac or a T-intersection or at the end of a straight road. A windmill or whirligig can raise the chi when placed outside a dwelling that is below street level. Note, however, that a dwelling below street level is not recommended, and if you live in one, it is best to move.

Moving water creates an excellent flow of chi, especially with regard to finances. Fountains and sculptures with an element of moving water are ideal. For a fountain in front of your home or business, be sure that the water flows straight up or points toward your front door, not away from your building. You don't need to keep the fountain on twenty-four hours a day, but do maintain it in good repair so that any time it is operated it works well.

Energy or fire-producing objects, such as fireplaces, stoves, and firecrackers, add emphasis and the strength of the fire element. Electrically charged objects, such as air conditioners, televisions, stereo systems, and computers, also add much chi. Sometimes too many electrically charged objects in the Lake/children area can overstimulate children. Use electrical objects with discretion and an awareness of the electromagnetic force fields. One way to temper the power of electronic equipment is to hang a crystal ball over it to break up the intense chi.

A classic feng shui solution to impart beauty and enhance chi is the use of artistic decorative objects that bring harmony and peace. Chinese bamboo flutes, simple landscape paintings, exquisite calligraphy, and other pieces of fine art have been treasured for centuries. Remove all art that depicts ugly, violent, or abstract chaotic imagery. Pretty multicolored fabric strips can be attached to ventilation and air-conditioning units so that they blow in the breeze from the vent like a mobile. Red silk tassels add a lovely decorative element and can be hung from door handles in areas where too many doors are grouped together.

Beautiful color can completely transform an area, especially when the colors correlate to the eight trigrams of the ba-gua. Rules regarding the use of color are explained in the *Book of Rites,* a classic Han dynasty text of Zhou customs. For example, in imperial buildings walls were red, roofs were yellow, pillars were deep scarlet, and staircases, terraces, and balustrades were white.

Each of the five elements exists in either a yang or a yin state. These five elements, with either yang or yin qualities, are called the "ten heavenly stems." Each stem is assigned a color depending on its element and gender, with yang being masculine and yin being feminine.

> Fire: yang fire is RED, and yin fire is PURPLE.
> Earth: yang earth is YELLOW, and yin earth is GOLD.
> Metal: yang metal is WHITE, and yin metal is SILVER.
> Water: yang water is BLACK, and yin water is GRAY.
> Wood: yang wood is GREEN, and yin wood is BLUE.

Yang colors represent the directional gua points (north, south, east, west) for each of the five elements.

Red, yang fire, is best suited to the Fire/fame gua. Bright red is a favored color in feng shui. It is the color of life, luck, happiness, prosperity, power, and glory. Yang colors are used in their purest and most brilliant form—Chinese red is famous the world over for its vibrancy and life-affirming qualities. Red is thought to ward off evil, and for this reason good-luck characters are written

YANG COLORS RELATED TO THE ELEMENTS

Red: yang fire
Fire/fame

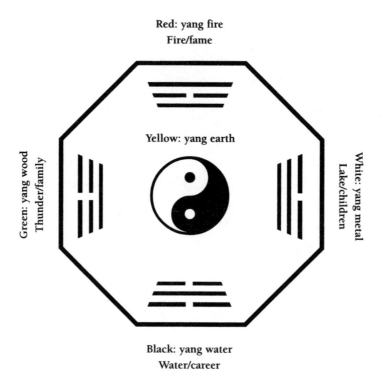

Green: yang wood
Thunder/family

Yellow: yang earth

White: yang metal
Lake/children

Black: yang water
Water/career

on red paper at the New Year. Red is symbolic of virtue and truth. Front doors are often painted red to establish power and guarantee protection.

White, yang metal, in the Lake/children gua represents purity and innocence. White also symbolizes moral and spiritual purity, like the Buddhist symbol of the white lotus flower. The lotus is white and pure even though it grows out of murky water. In China and the rest of Asia, white is the color of death and mourning (unlike the West, where black represents mourning). Children are celebrated as the continuation of life.

Black, yang water, is the color of the career gua, the color of deep waters and the darkness of winter. Black, navy blue, or deep blue can be used in this area. Black is not always favored, since many demons are depicted as black, the color of bruises. Yet very black ink is used in Chinese art, and the color symbolizes seriousness and justice.

YIN COLORS RELATED TO THE ELEMENTS

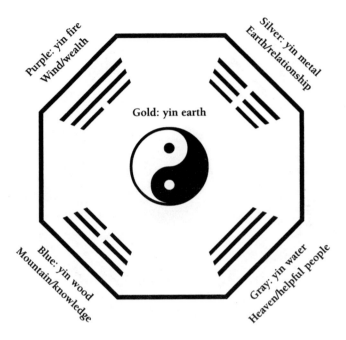

Gold: yin earth

Purple: yin fire
Wind/wealth

Silver: yin metal
Earth/relationship

Blue: yin wood
Mountain/knowledge

Gray: yin water
Heaven/helpful people

Green, yang wood, is the color of the Thunder/family gua. It stands for lush growth, vegetation, and rebirth in springtime, and it is the color of the valued gemstone jade. Jade comes in many colors, but green jade is most treasured. Early Chinese porcelains were decorated with green glazes to imitate jade. Green represents hope, longevity, and vitality.

Yellow, yang earth, is located in the center of the ba-gua. The symbolic use of color in China can indicate authority and rank. Yellow is China's national color, and it was the color of the emperor, his sons, and those of his lineage. (Although purple was the color of the emperor's grandsons.) Tibetan Buddhist monks and priests also wear yellow because it represents their spiritual life. Yellow is associated with the traits of tolerance, acceptance, honesty, and trustworthiness.

The yin guas lie between the directional yang gua points and are exemplified by the yin colors of each of the five elements.

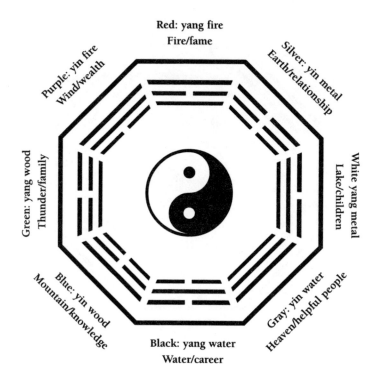

Purple, yin fire, is the color of the Wind/wealth gua. The Chinese saying "It is so red that it's purple" means that a dark, intense red looks purple. Purple has a function similar to red and can be used in this gua with red and gold to represent wealth. Purple is associated with royalty and pageantry. At one time, purple dye was so rare and costly that only the rich and royal could afford it.

Blue, yin wood, is appropriate in the Mountain/knowledge gua because blue is a calming, peaceful color for meditation and contemplation. Blue represents blessings.

Gray, yin water, is a color composed of black and white. The Heaven/helpful people gua is located between black water and white metal, giving it a connection to both of those realms.

Silver, yin metal, is used in the Earth/relationship gua. It is a color close to the white of Lake/children, but Earth/relationship is also represented by the color pink because pink is a combination of red and white. Pink is used extensively in this area to attract relationships and is associated with love and affection.

Gold, yin earth, lies at the center. Gilt and gold are symbols of wealth and prosperity, like red. The walls of the forbidden city in Beijing are decorated with red, and the roofs are gold. (Note that "gold" is occasionally used as a translation for the element metal.)

Together, the yang and yin manifestations of all five elements in balance create the ten heavenly stems of feng shui ba-gua.

Colored crystal balls can be hung in each gua according to color. For example, sapphire is best in the Mountain/knowledge gua, as is emerald in the Thunder/family gua. Rose works in the Earth/relationship gua. A crystal ball that does not have a hole for hanging can be placed in a stand or holder. Put a small mirror under the crystal in a stand to create a double image in the Earth/relationship gua.

Mindfully embellish each gua in your home and office as if you were creating an altar. An altar is a place for material objects that hold spiritual significance for you and that represent your inner self. An altar can be made on a tabletop, dresser, or any flat surface. We decorate by unconsciously making altars and refer to them as "interior design." Use the design of your interior—your inner dreams and symbols—to embellish each gua.

Fire/Fame

Incorporate the color of fire—red, purple, and orange. This gua must be well lit and never dark or dingy. Symbols of achievement, such as a framed diploma, are appropriately placed in this gua. One of my clients, born in the year of the Serpent, is an Emmy-winning director. He keeps his Emmy statue in the Fire/fame gua of his office. Even better than an Emmy is a fireplace or heater. Fireplaces add the element fire in the perfect fire location. If a window is in this gua, hang a large crystal ball or three small crystal balls for emphasis. Lush plants, red flowers, and artificial fruit-bearing trees with red fruit impart chi, because wood feeds fire. Do not place a fountain or fish tank in this gua because water extinguishes fire. Do not build a fountain or center a pool in the rear of your backyard, since this area is the Fire/fame gua of your property. Instead, add a red fence and trees.

Earth/Relationship

Embellish this gua in all rooms, especially your bedroom. Keep your bedroom clean and be sure that your bed is in the commanding position and facing the mouth of chi. Mirrors are recommended in this gua, especially those that are round or oval yin shapes. Use the color pink, including pink sheets and pink flowers. This is the perfect gua for wedding pictures or pictures of your romantic partner. A fireplace is also fine because fire nurtures the element earth. A computer or television is not suited to this gua, nor is this a good location for a pet area. If you favor your pet here, the pet may become your primary partner. A bathroom is not ideally located in the Earth/relationship gua of the home. But if it is situated there, decorate it in pink tones and place a plant potted in a pink or red container on the toilet. If you remain forlorn about lack of love over a long period of time, move.

Heaven/Helpful People

In this gua belong images of high spiritual beings who can assist you, such as a statue of the Buddha, pictures of angels, a bust of a leader, or an embroidered dragon's head or picture of a dragon, which symbolizes leadership. A fountain or aquarium is superb in this gua. Pictures of friends who can help you are fine, but baby pictures are not appropriate in this gua because a baby needs to be nurtured. Crystals and wind chimes in this area can attract positive helpers. A computer can help find travel information or other networking resources.

Water/Career

Since this gua is usually located at the mouth of chi, it must be kept clean and free of clutter. If guests remove their footware when entering, purchase a small cabinet to contain the footware. This cabinet should not be a storage area for your shoes as well, because it will take up too much space and block the entrance. Indoors, art depicting waterfalls, dolphins, coi fish, or other watery imagery is appropriate. The art should not picture disturbing or turbulent images, such as huge waves or ships tossed at sea. This is the best gua in which to place a computer to maintain career prosperity. A water fountain located in this gua of the front yard stimulates the water element and creates prosperity. Be sure that the fountain does not block the front door.

Wind/Wealth

The colors of wealth—red, purple, and gold—are appropriate for this gua. Pictures of a golden Buddha, a waterfall, or fishermen with nets bursting with fish are all symbols of money and prosperity. A fountain or aquarium is an excellent addition to this gua. Flowers, bamboo, and lush plants with round leaves, such as a jade plant or a rubber tree, are also positive embellishments. Remember that mirrors are not suited to this gua. A computer in this area can be the source for updated financial information. A fireplace is not appropriate because it may symbolically burn money. One solution is to hang a large mirror over the fireplace, not use the fireplace, and put three or nine large plants around it to soften the chi. Ventilation or an air-conditioning unit is not ideally placed here if it blows outside, since it symbolically blows away money. In your business, locate your cash register in this gua. If you cannot, place it in the Heaven/helpful people gua instead. Do not put it in the Lake/children gua, to avoid childish handling of finances. Place a red cloth under your register and hang a large crystal ball from the ceiling over it. Do not position the register so that you turn your back to your customers after you take their money.

A bathroom is not well placed in the Wind/wealth gua, because money will go down the drain. Possible solutions are to decorate the bathroom in the color purple, place a healthy plant in a red container on the toilet, and affix small circular mirrors from the ceiling over the drains of the toilet, sink, and bath. If debts keep accruing, move. A fountain, pool, birdbath, or fishpond are excellent additions to the Wind/wealth gua of your property. Be sure that the water is kept clean and not allowed to become overgrown with algae.

Mountain/Knowledge

This is your personal area for reflection and self-development, a place to sit, relax, read, and meditate. An altar or a bookcase filled with books is very well placed in this area. Enhance this gua with a bright light, mirror, or crystal ball to add illumination, or use moving objects, such as a wind chime or a mobile, to keep this area active in your life. Fresh flowers and lush plants are symbolic of fresh ideas and new mental and spiritual growth. Dried flowers and wreaths are especially undesirable in this gua. The energy-producing items that create difficulties in other guas—computer, fireplace, television, and stereo—are fine here. A computer in this gua can be used to acquire new knowledge. A fireplace adds vitality to inner development. A television can open doors to learning. A stereo enhances spiritual growth inspired by music. It is helpful to place potted plants within a three-foot radius of the television or stereo to lessen the electromagnetic force field.

This gua is an important focal point in outdoor landscaping. One client landscaped a beautiful shaded Zen meditation grove in this area of his yard. It included a Buddha statue placed amidst a grouping of stones that he had collected over the years, a comfortable swinging bench, a large brass wind chime hung in a pine tree behind the bench, and two statues of fu dogs that protected the entrance to his meditation grove. A little creek that ran behind the grove added a sense of mystery. Although his yard included a swimming pool, vegetable garden, barbecue, and sauna, this unassuming little grove was the most inviting area of the yard because of the refined and spiritual chi contained there. Make sure that this area is not cluttered, indoors and out, for that could parallel a cluttered mind.

Thunder/Family

The importance of this gua is that it can keep your family strong and unified. This area also influences your family's fate. This is the ideal location for family photographs, heirlooms, and an altar to one's ancestors. Lush plants and the color green work well in this gua, which corresponds to the element wood. As the plants grow, the family grows. Plants that wither in this gua must be removed and replaced to maintain your family's health. All of the items used in effecting feng shui corrections are appropriate for this gua, especially sound, symbolizing the voice of ancestors. Ventilation, however, is not appropriate because it carries the symbolic image of a family breaking apart and scattering. A computer is not well placed in this area, the place of reverence to ancestors. When there is discord within a family, focus attention to this area of the home to bring about a peaceful outcome.

Lake/Children

Mindfully embellish this gua in your child's room and in the living room to help your child when she stumbles in life. To gain understanding of your child's perception, walk through her room on your knees. Note what is at eye level and add feng shui solutions from this perspective. For example, hang a mirror to reflect your child's face at her own height. Walking on your knees can also be done in a classroom to design the space according to a child's outlook. A desk is fine in a child's bedroom because schoolwork is a large part of a child's life. But it is not advisable to place a desk in an adult's bedroom because it may cause an adult to overwork. To enhance your sensitivity as a parent, decorate the Lake/children gua in your own bedroom. This is the place for photographs of children, baby pictures, and toys.

A sick child can be helped by placing plants in his room specifically in this gua. White flowers are recommended because this area corresponds to the element metal. If you dislike using fresh flowers because the flowers die, use stuffed animals. It is not wise to have a fireplace in this gua because it may overstimulate children. If there is one, add nine plants around the fireplace to lessen its influence and hang a large mirror over the fireplace so that the water influence will extinguish the fire.

Ventilation and air conditioners do not create positive chi in this gua. Move the air conditioner. If a vent cannot be relocated, tie colored streamers to it so that they dance in the wind when the vent is on. This gua represents both your children and your own creativity. This is the place for your items of personal expression. A painter would do well to place an easel here, a writer to place a desk, or a musician to place instruments and recording equipment. Just be sure that you are not engaging in a creative act in the direct line of chi if the room is entered from the Heaven/helpful people gua. Do your creative work in the commanding position. All feng shui solutions can work well here, especially those that are fun and add color.

Be conscious of your application of feng shui solutions. Be grateful for the opportunity to create change in your life. According to feng shui master Professor Lin Yun Rinpoche, a transformational way to apply feng shui solutions is to utilize the "three secrets of reinforcement" to strengthen your solutions and manifest your goals. His three secrets are the use of hand gesutures, prayer, and visualization.

Hand gestures are called *mudras* in Sanskrit. The influence of Buddhism in Chinese culture brought in the use of hand postures as part of prayer. These can be seen in religious Buddhist art, as in the hand positions of the Buddha. In the West, the prayer gesture of both hands held together at chest level is a form of mudra. A peaceful hand gesture for you to try is to nestle the back of your left fingers into your right palm. Your right fingers support the back of your left hand. Allow the tips of your thumbs to touch. Sit with your hands in this mudra and gently focus on your breathing. Feel each

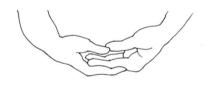

inhalation and each exhalation, like the dance of yin and yang. As you sit more quietly, focus within to hear your heartbeat. You may be surprised to learn how much it sounds like a drumbeat. After sitting in this meditative posture, begin your feng shui corrections. To banish, oust, or remove sha chi, push your middle and ring fingers away from your thumb as if flicking off water. After putting a feng shui embellishment in place, return your hands to the peaceful meditation pose or place them together at your chest in the Western prayer position, to help you concentrate on your solution.

Prayer is the second secret of reinforcement. Speak words of peace while you are applying your feng shui solutions. Do not utter inappropriate or angry words, which could have a negative effect on what you are trying to achieve. If you are hanging a wind chime in the Thunder/family gua of your yard to disperse difficulties with in-laws, do not curse them. Behave with respect and appreciation for the opportunity to effect a feng shui correction. Speak holy words that have meaning for you. One client recited the Lord's Prayer nine times because that prayer had been her favorite since childhood. Another client, a recovering alcoholic, recited the serenity prayer because it held great meaning for her. You can repeat a word that applies to a particular solution, such as "peace," "love," or "transformation." A Buddhist prayer in Sanskrit calls on the "beauty in the heart of the lotus" through the six perfect syllables "om mani padme hum."

The third secret is to visualize, meaning to see in your mind's eye the positive outcome of applying your feng shui solutions. See the magic before it happens! Picture your outcome so strongly that you can actually *feel* it coming about. Concentrate on your visualization so that your mind does not picture a fearful situation or focus on negative thoughts. Be prepared to repeat your visualization many times. For example, if you are visualizing a loving partnership while adding a mirror in the Earth/relationship gua, note the thoughts that creep through even though you are reciting a prayer out loud. Does your visualization become scattered when fearful thoughts surface? Allow them to pass like clouds and begin your visualization again. A teaching of the Buddha states, "We are what we think. All that we are arises with our thoughts. With our thoughts we make the world."

Do not simply hang a mirror. Instead, speak holy words while you are hanging the mirror. Think only about what you are doing and why. Visualize the best possible outcome. After the mirror is hung, hold your hands in a prayerful position, still concentrating on your solution, and keep on reciting your holy words. At first it may be challenging to put all three secrets of reinforcement into play at the same time, but you will improve with practice.

EIGHT

Reckoning of Fate

THE ANCIENT TAOISTS were brilliant and wise astronomers and astrologers. As early as 4000 B.C., the sages developed astronomy through careful observation of the heavens. By the year 2000 B.C., they had created an agricultural calendar, recognized constellations that guided them in their travels, determined that the length of a year was 365¼ days, and were able to predict solar and lunar eclipses. They recorded Halley's comet in 467 B.C. The ancient Taoists were the first to recognize that the moon moves eastward in relation to the stars in a twenty-eight-day cycle.

Taoist astrology, or *ming shu* ("the reckoning of fate"), is unique among all astrological systems. Ming shu is structured on a twelve-year cycle, each year named for one of the twelve zodiac animals: Rat, Ox, Tiger, Hare, Dragon, Serpent, Horse, Sheep, Monkey, Phoenix (Rooster), Dog, and Boar. This twelve-year cycle is repeated five times, each time for one of the five elements—fire, earth, metal, water, and wood. The combination of the twelve animals with the five elements in their yin and yang states results in continuous sixty-year cycles. Each sixty-year cycle starts in a fire Rat year. The most recent sixty-year cycle began on the new moon of February 19, 1996 (the year 4694 in the Chinese calendar).

The Chinese New Year begins on the second new moon after the winter solstice, not on January 1 of the Gregorian calendar. The Chinese New Year is a time to visit family and friends, to prepare luscious feasts, and to celebrate until the full moon fifteen days later, when the New Year festivities culminate in a parade. Also celebrated on the day of the full moon is the lantern festival. Beautiful lanterns are created from bamboo, wood, silk, and paper and are used in the New Year festivities. In ancient times the lantern festival was a fertility rite that celebrated the return of the sun's light after the cold of winter.

The Chinese New Year is an auspicious time to foster good luck and to pay respect to the gods, goddesses, and spirits. The folk tradition of sending messages to the kitchen god indicates the importance of the stove (hearth) as the soul of a home. Clean stoves in good working order guarantee peace and good fortune. Dirty or malfunctioning stoves can bring strife and misunderstanding. To ensure positive feng shui for the coming year, homes and businesses are cleaned, clutter is removed, and old clothes are replaced with new clothes. Any piece of furniture that has stood in one place during the year is moved to clean the area around it. What is considered "spring cleaning" in the West is done the week before the Chinese New Year to ensure a lucky new beginning. The color red is always used in the New Year celebrations because it is considered a fortunate color. Red is the color to paint a door to frighten away demons. If you do not have an element of red by your front door, the New Year holiday is a good time to add it.

The Chinese New Year is celebrated at some time between mid-January and mid-February on the Gregorian calendar. February 2, the first day of spring according to the Chinese, can be considered either the beginning of the year or the end of the year. A year without the first day of spring is a "blind" year. During years that are not blind, conditions are more favorable for marriage, the birth of children, investing in property, and buying or expanding a business. For example, the year of the yellow earth Tiger (1998) is considered very auspicious, since it began on January 28 and ended on February 15. The first day of spring occurs at both the "nose" and the "tail" of this Tiger. The year of the gold earth Hare (1999) is not blind because it ended on February 4, but the year of the white metal Dragon (2000) is a blind year, since it began on February 5 and ended on January 23. Refer to the appendix to determine which years are blind. Supplemental feng shui solutions are often required for properties purchased or buildings constructed during blind years. Properties and projects also assume the characteristics of the animal year in which they were started. The following tale indicates the problems that can surface during a blind year.

In 1997, the year of the purple fire Ox, a couple both born in the red fire Horse year purchased a lovely old home in San Francisco. They planned to occupy their new home in April, but first the building needed to comply with a city earthquake code requiring seismic retrofitting. The retrofitting was to take about a week to complete. A vast pit was dug around the home to reinforce the foundation, but the pit promptly filled with rain from an unexpected storm. After the pit was dredged, another el Niño storm again swamped it. The red fire Horses were chomping at the bit to move in. Instead, they spent money to live in a hotel, while making their first mortgage payments. They also paid to store their belongings. Meanwhile, their contractor's bill kept growing. The laborious Ox influence continued to slow the project. More storms came. Finally, after numerous stumbling blocks, the couple finally occupied their new home in November. To avoid your own blind complications, thoroughly examine all the ways in which there can be chi imbalances. Be especially diligent about legal proceedings and responsibilities, which the red fire Horses, in their rush to purchase their dream home, did not do.

Feng shui solutions can be tailored to your Taoist animal sign. Your sign is determined by your year of birth—unlike the Western system, in which your sign is determined by the month of your birth. Knowing your sign can offer much insight into personality traits, relationship compatibility, parent and child relationships, and cycles of rising and falling fortunes. Discover your astrological sign by finding your year of birth on the following chart. If you were born in January or February, refer to the appendix for the correct year.

Rat: 1900, 1912, 1924, 1936, 1948, 1960, 1972, 1984, 1996, 2008, 2020

Ox: 1901, 1913, 1925, 1937, 1949, 1961, 1973, 1985, 1997, 2009, 2021

Tiger: 1902, 1914, 1926, 1938, 1950, 1962, 1974, 1986, 1998, 2010, 2022

Hare: 1903, 1915, 1927, 1939, 1951, 1963, 1975, 1987, 1999, 2011, 2023

Dragon: 1904, 1916, 1928, 1940, 1952, 1964, 1976, 1988, 2000, 2012, 2024

Serpent: 1905, 1917, 1929, 1941, 1953, 1965, 1977, 1989, 2001, 2013, 2025

Horse: 1906, 1918, 1930, 1942, 1954, 1966, 1978, 1990, 2002, 2014, 2026

Sheep: 1907, 1919, 1931, 1943, 1955, 1967, 1979, 1991, 2003, 2015, 2027

Monkey: 1908, 1920, 1932, 1944, 1956, 1968, 1980, 1992, 2004, 2016, 2028

Phoenix: 1909, 1921, 1933, 1945, 1957, 1969, 1981, 1993, 2005, 2017, 2029

Dog: 1910, 1922, 1934, 1946, 1958, 1970, 1982, 1994, 2006, 2018, 2030

Boar: 1911, 1923, 1935, 1947, 1959, 1971, 1983, 1995, 2007, 2019, 2031

The twelve animal signs are grouped in four harmony triads that determine relationship compatibility. The three animals that share your harmony trine, or group of three, are most compatible because they possess similar values, ideals, and goals. These triads also indicate the auspicious years for your animal signs.

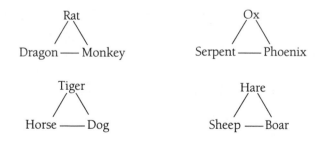

You are incompatible with the animal sign that is your opposite in the twelve-year cycle. There is a six-year age difference between you and your incompatible opposite. Ironically, though, it is from our opposites that we learn and achieve success by integrating their qualities into our character. In this way, the balance of the Tao is maintained.

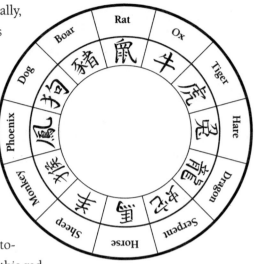

One feng shui solution to create harmony among all twelve signs is to collect a little statue of each animal sign and string all twelve of them together with a red ribbon. Hang this red ribbon in the hallway of an apartment building, in the kitchen of a restaurant, in the Water/career gua of an office, or in a living room in the Thunder/family gua—wherever harmony needs to be fostered among strangers, coworkers, or family members.

The twelve animal signs, also known as the "twelve earthly branches," are based on seasonal cycles.

鼠 Rat

The first earthly branch occurs when yang chi emerges during the winter solstice. The yang sun starts to return, and the days grow longer. This is the time of cold and snow, when seeds deep in the soil begin to germinate. This first earthly branch represents December, the eleventh month in the Chinese lunar calendar. December is the time of Sagittarius, Rat's Western counterpart. Since this is the first earthly branch, the ability to be first in all things is a Rat trait.

The best years for a Rat to marry, have a child, or expect doors of opportunity to open are Dragon, Serpent, and Monkey years. Rat's luckiest months are the third, seventh, and twelfth lunar months. Rat's best days are the eleventh day of the seventh lunar month and the twelfth day of the twelfth lunar month. A bad day for Rats and an unfortunate day for marriage is the fifth day of the fifth lunar month. When figuring these dates, remember that the first lunar month starts on the Chinese New Year, the second new moon after winter solstice. Horse years are not lucky for Rat.

The ba-gua focus for Rat should be the Water/career and the Wind/wealth guas because clever Rat thrives on success. Rat's earthly branch is of the element water, so it is important that Rat's work bring fulfillment. Rats often accumulate wealth as a result of being the first in all things and applying their Rat ingenuity and intelligence. Rats tend to hoard, especially the yellow earth Rat. Pay attention to removing clutter from all ba-gua locations.

牛 Ox

The second earthly branch occurs when yin chi disappears completely and is replaced by yang chi. The seed struggles to sprout and break through the earth. This determination and perseverance are Ox qualities. The second earthly branch represents January, the twelfth lunar month. January is the time of Capricorn, Ox's Western counterpart.

The best years for the Ox to marry, have a child, or expect doors of opportunity to open are Rat, Serpent, and Phoenix years. Ox's luckiest months are the fourth, eighth, and eleventh lunar months. Ox's best days are the eighth day of the fourth lunar month and the eleventh day of the eleventh lunar month. A bad day for Ox and an unfortunate day for marriage is the sixth day of the sixth lunar month. Sheep years are not lucky for Ox.

The ba-gua focus for the honest Ox should be stability of the Water/career gua, but for reasons different from the Rat's. Ox diligently applies much energy to completing tasks. In a competitive work environment, Ox may be overlooked when promotions are given to clever Rats and Monkeys or dynamic Dragons and Tigers. To guarantee that Ox is rewarded for hard work, a solid and balanced Water/career gua is helpful. Family security is also very important to Ox, so the Thunder/family gua and the Lake/children gua should be embellished.

虎 Tiger

The third earthly branch occurs as yang chi develops. The new sprout bursts with life force and vitality. Those born in a Tiger year share the same positive and upward-reaching qualities as a growing sprout. The third earthly branch represents February, the first lunar month. February is the time of Aquarius, Tiger's Western counterpart.

The best years for the Tiger to marry, have a child, or expect doors of opportunity to open are Horse, Dog, and Boar years. Tiger's luckiest months are the first, ninth, and tenth lunar months. Tiger's best days are the fifth day of the first or ninth lunar month and the tenth day of the tenth lunar month. A bad day for Tigers and an unfortunate day for marriage is the seventh day of the seventh lunar month. Monkey years are not lucky for Tiger.

The ba-gua focus for the eager Tiger should be the Lake/children gua, to encourage development of artistic creative expression. In this sense, "children" also refers to what we create (our works of art are also children). A Tiger who is not free to express creatively is like a Tiger in a cage. This gua corresponds to the element metal. Because Tiger can act impulsively without reflection, embellishment of the Mountain/knowledge gua is also helpful.

兔 Hare

The fourth earthly branch occurs as yang chi continues to grow strong. Plants grow effortlessly and quickly in warm spring light. The gentle qualities of springtime are traits of those born in the year of the Hare. The fourth earthly branch represents March, the second lunar month. March is the time of Pisces, Hare's Western counterpart.

The best years for the Hare to marry, have a child, or expect doors of opportunity to open are Sheep, Dog, and Boar years. Hare's luckiest months are the sixth, ninth, and tenth lunar months. Hare's best days are the ninth day of the ninth lunar month and the second day of the tenth lunar month. A bad day for Hares and an unfortunate day for marriage is the eighth day of the eighth lunar month. Phoenix years are not lucky for Hare.

The ba-gua focus for the peace-loving Hare should be the Earth/relationship gua. Hare desires refinement and harmony in all interactions with others. Hare becomes upset, even ill, when others do not behave in a gracious and harmonious manner. By cultivating the peaceful qualities of the yin and fertile earth,

Hare creates a charmed circle of partners, friends, family, and coworkers.

龍 Dragon

The fifth earthly branch occurs when yang chi is robust. Plants grow vigorously. This powerful and hearty chi characterizes those born in the year of the Dragon. The fifth earthly branch represents April, the third lunar month. April is the time of Aries, Dragon's Western counterpart.

The best years for Dragon to marry, have a child, or expect doors of opportunity to open are Rat, Monkey, and Phoenix years. Dragon's luckiest months are the third, seventh, eighth, and eleventh lunar months. Dragon's best days are the eleventh day of the seventh lunar month and the eighth day of the eighth lunar month. A bad day for Dragons and an unfortunate day for marriage is the ninth day of the ninth lunar month. Dog years are not lucky for Dragon.

The ba-gua focus for the mighty Dragon should be the Fire/fame gua; this area should include the color red. Mighty Dragons desire acclaim and respect from everyone who orbits their world. According to the five-element theory, the wood element should also be enhanced because wood is Dragon's earthly branch and wood feeds fire, helping Dragon succeed and attain the recognition that Dragon commands. Strong wood is an absolute necessity for the green wood Dragon.

蛇 Serpent

The sixth earthly branch occurs as yang chi peaks and then becomes yin. Plants have completed their growth. This turning point brings the outward growth inward, transforming vigor and power into wisdom. These characteristics are reflected in those born in the year of the Serpent. The sixth earthly branch symbolizes May, the fourth lunar month. May is the time of Taurus, Serpent's Western counterpart.

The best years for Serpent to marry, have a child, or expect doors of opportunity to open are Ox, Monkey, and Phoenix years. Serpent's luckiest months are the fourth, seventh, eighth, and twelfth lunar months. Serpent's best days are the eighth day of the fourth lunar month and the seventh day of the seventh lunar month. A bad day for Serpents and an unfortunate day for marriage is the tenth day of the tenth lunar month. Boar years are not lucky for Serpent.

The ba-gua focus for the contemplative Serpent should be the Mountain/knowledge gua. If this area of life is cultivated, the wise Serpent can develop the innate awareness to act in harmony with the Tao. To create a void in which to place new understanding—the hollow cave of the mountain—Serpent must shed the skins of the past. The Thunder/family gua is important for Serpent because the shedding of skin symbolizes the birth of the next generation and the importance of what we learn from our elders and pass on to our children. Serpents must remove clutter often. They tend to block stairways and the mouth of chi to rooms, creating an environment that only a Serpent can slither through to enter. The Fire/fame gua must be controlled and modulated for summer-born Serpents to curb ruthless behavior.

馬 Horse

The seventh earthly branch occurs when there is still relatively powerful yang chi but yin chi has started to settle in. The sun is brightest, and the plants are strong, having reached maturity. Those born in Horse years possess a sunny disposition and are bright, open, and cheerful. The seventh earthly branch symbolizes June, the fifth lunar month. June is the time of Gemini, Horse's Western counterpart.

The best years for Horse to marry, have a child, or expect doors of opportunity to open are Tiger, Sheep, and Dog years. Horse's luckiest months are the first, sixth, and ninth lunar months. Horse's best days are the fifth day of the ninth lunar month and the sixth day of the sixth lunar month. A bad day for Horses and an unfortunate day for marriage is the eleventh day of the eleventh lunar month. Rat years are not lucky for Horse.

The ba-gua focus for the expressive Horse should be the Lake/children gua, to help Horse have more fun and enjoy life in a free, childlike manner. Horse often succeeds after others intervene to offer guidance; for this reason, a focus on the Heaven/helpful people gua is also important for Horse, especially during youth. Horse's earthly branch is the element fire. In the five-element theory, developing the wood element helps brighten Horse's natural fiery soul essence, but for those born in the year of the red fire Horse, the fire element is best if modified. This type of Horse benefits greatly from developing the Mountain/knowledge gua, to learn to be introspective.

羊 Sheep

The eighth earthly branch occurs when the mature plant bears fruit; all is peaceful, and yin grows strong. This gentle, peaceful yin essence is the core of Sheep's nature. The eighth earthly branch symbolizes July, the sixth lunar month. July is the time of Cancer, Sheep's Western counterpart.

The best years for Sheep to marry, have a child, or expect doors of opportunity to open are Hare, Horse, and Boar years. Sheep's luckiest months are the fifth, sixth, and tenth lunar months. Sheep's best days are the second day of the tenth lunar month and the fifth day of the fifth lunar month. A bad day for Sheep and an unfortunate day for marriage is the twelfth day of the twelfth lunar month. Ox years are not lucky for Sheep.

The ba-gua focus for the kind and gentle Sheep should be an overall balance of all eight trigram locations. Being a peaceful flock animal, the Earth/relationship gua is important to the Sheep individual. Sheep have a natural capacity to understand the Thunder/family gua—even lambs demonstrate correct reverence for their elders when they kneel before their mother to nurse. Sheep also have an affinity for Mountain/knowledge because the Sheep enjoys solitary reflective movements to restore the soul and find peace. Those born in the gray water Sheep year are bettered when the Heaven/helpful people gua is strengthened, since they benefit from strong guidance. All ba-gua embellishments for Sheep must be in the best taste—no tacky wind chimes or gaudy fountains for these artistic connoisseurs.

猴 Monkey

The ninth earthly branch occurs when crops are ready to harvest. That is why Monkeys naturally have so many developed talents and abilities. The ninth branch symbolizes August, the seventh lunar month. August is the time of Leo, Monkey's Western counterpart.

The best years for Monkey to marry, have a child, or expect doors of opportunity to open are Rat, Dragon, and Serpent years. Monkey's luckiest months are the third, fourth, seventh, and tenth lunar months. Monkey's best days are the eleventh day of the seventh lunar month and the fourth day of the fourth lunar month. A bad day for Monkeys and an unfortunate day for marriage is the first day of the first lunar month. Tiger years are not lucky for Monkey.

The ba-gua focus for Monkey is similar to the Dragon's. Emphasis is on the Fire/fame area. Embellishments include liberal use of the color red and large mirrors. The individualistic Monkey is successful in life and can achieve great goals regardless of obstacles. The more fame and recognition that Monkeys receive for their wild schemes and innovative concepts, the more they are inspired to accomplish and create. Also of importance is the position opposite Fire/fame—the gua of Water/career. Monkeys apply more of their ingenious wit and dynamic energy to a career that they find personally satisfying.

鳳 Phoenix

The tenth earthly branch occurs during harvest, as yang chi is weakened but yin chi is strengthened and rejuvenated. Satisfaction for work well done and potential for rejuvenation characterize those born in the year of the Phoenix. The tenth earthly branch symbolizes September, the eighth lunar month. September is the time of Virgo, Phoenix's Western counterpart.

The best years for Phoenix to marry, have a child, or expect doors of opportunity to open are Ox, Dragon, and Serpent years. Phoenix's luckiest months are the third, fourth, eighth, and twelfth lunar months. Phoenix's best days are the eighth day of the fourth lunar month and the third day of the third lunar month. A bad day for Phoenix and an unfortunate day for marriage is the second day of the second lunar month. Hare years are not lucky for Phoenix.

The ba-gua focus for the thrifty Phoenix should be the Wind/wealth gua. Acquiring, spending, and investing money offers Phoenix a sense of security and power. Once those born in the year of the Phoenix feel secure, they can make a powerful contribution to humanity as healers and helpers. Because Phoenix's eccentric personality often clashes with others, embellishment of the Earth/relationship gua helps ease the path to harmonious interactions, especially with coworkers. Learning to interact peaceably with others is most important for the purple fire Phoenix.

狗 Dog

The eleventh earthly branch occurs as plants wither, animals prepare for winter, and yin chi gains strength. This ability to diligently prepare and be responsible are qualities of those born in the year of the Dog. The eleventh earthly branch symbolizes October, the ninth lunar month. October is the time of Libra, Dog's Western counterpart.

The best years for Dog to marry, have a child, or expect doors of opportunity to open are Tiger, Hare, and Horse years. Dog's luckiest months are the first, fifth, and ninth lunar months. Dog's best day is the fifth day of the first lunar month. A bad day for Dogs and an unfortunate day for marriage is the third day of the third lunar month. Dragon years are not lucky for Dog.

The ba-gua focus for Dog should be the Water/career location, because Dogs believe passionately in what they do. If Dogs are compromised in their career choice, they suffer until the problem is corrected. The red fire Dog and the white metal Dog can temper fanaticism by cultivating the element water. Also of importance for Dog is the Thunder/family gua, which inspires Dog's sense of loyalty. In the five-element theory, metal is Dog's earthly branch—symbolic representation of metal is important in the environment of the dog.

豬 Boar

The twelfth earthly branch occurs as yin chi strengthens externally and yang chi draws inward. Earth is at rest in winter, and a sense of peacefulness is prevalent. Love of rest and cultivation of peace are Boar qualities. The twelfth earthly branch symbolizes November, the tenth lunar month. November is the time of Scorpio, Boar's Western counterpart.

The best years for a Boar to marry, have a child, or expect doors of opportunity to open are Tiger, Hare, and Sheep years. Boar's luckiest months are the first, sixth, and tenth lunar months. Boar's best days are the first day of the first lunar month and the sixth day of both the sixth and tenth lunar months. A bad day for Boars and an unfortunate day for marriage is the fourth day of the fourth lunar month.

The ba-gua focus for the kindhearted Boar should be the Heaven/helpful people gua, so that Boar can find support from others and not be taken advantage of. Like Hare, Boar should also emphasize the Earth/relationship gua to create a special intimate circle of kind partners, friends, family, and coworkers who will cherish Boar. Like Sheep, pay attention to the overall balance of every trigram position, because all Boars can be indulgent when moderation is required, especially the golden earth Boar and the gray water Boar.

Organize the feng shui of your home and office to reflect your birth year element as well as the best ba-gua focus for your animal sign. Do not neglect your birth year element!

Before I enter the home or office of a feng shui client, I know what to expect because when I schedule our appointment, I ask them their birth year. Their environment always reflects the qualities of their animal sign and birth year element.

A woman born in the year of the green wood Dragon had created too much wood in her environment. Her pine-paneled living room was full of large houseplants, including hanging baskets. The feeling was not one of a fertile jungle, but of a crowded environment. The simple solution was to remove most of the wood by keeping only a couple of the houseplants. They were placed next to a window in the Fire/fame area of the ba-gua because wood nurtures fire, and this gua is important for Dragons. In this way, wood was strongly represented in her environment, but in balance.

Too much earth in an environment translates as too much clutter. This was the case for a man born in the year of the yellow earth Dog. His feng shui solution was to remove clutter, recycle, clean out his closets, and raise his standard of housekeeping. Excessive earth resulted in stagnation of opportunities. He unblocked his chi by lessening the earth element through conscious clearing out of junk and clutter. His girlfriend decided to live with him after she saw that he could be cleaner. His relationship success was not due to embellishing his Earth/relationship gua. In this instance, he simply focused on balancing his birth element. Even though he had to move to a larger place for the both of them, he was very pleased. In quite a few instances, after clients who rent mindfully applied feng shui solutions to their homes, the elevation of chi opened the door for them to move to a better housing situation.

If your birth element is lacking, you may feel uneasy. This was the case when I arrived at the home of Kim, a woman born in 1961, the year of the silver metal Ox. I expected to find a serene, Zen-like clean home typical of the metal sensibility. Kim was very serious about her career, which did not surprise me since the ability to perform hard work is an Ox trait. I assumed that I would see an organized home office. Instead, I entered her living room to find that her work desk was covered in piles of paper and faced a blank wall, and many large potted plants were crammed into the living room. The first thing I did was explain how the flow of chi was blocked. She and I removed the plants from the living room and temporarily placed them in the hallway just for her to *feel* how the plants blocked the chi. Kim was amazed and told me that she bought this house because when she first entered it, it was vacant. She immediately felt at peace in the large, empty living room with blonde wood floors and a lovely view of the Berkeley hills. Ever since the day she moved in, Kim had unknowingly longed for that feeling of emptiness—the clean metal environment where her soul felt most at peace, and an orderly environment where an Ox could maintain a structured routine. She had some work to do to arrive at that point, but she was willing to clean up her clutter, move her desk to the commanding position facing the entry, recycle her papers, and give away almost all of her big plants. With each improvement her home was closer to feeling the way it did when she first saw it, when it was a metal environment.

Learn from Kim's experience and make sure that your birth year element is obviously present in your home and office. Also learn from the green wood Dragon example that too much can be overwhelming. Strive to represent your birth element in balance. For example, I was born in the year of the blue wood Sheep. My bedroom and living room contain a few large lush plants. But the rooms are not cluttered with many potted plants. Whenever I enter an environment without much wood, I feel as if vital chi is lacking and the air is stale. I am most content in a space where wood is represented, but represented in balance.

Whenever I recommend an indoor water fountain for the bedroom or living room Wind/wealth corner of clients born in a water year, they respond enthusiastically since water is their natural element. Whenever I recommend that fire types decorate their home in bright colors, such as light yellow walls in the living room and lavender walls in the bedroom, they respond enthusiastically. They benefit from the excitement and stimulation that fire brings. (Painting tip: choose the brightest and strongest colors that you like, but keep the ceiling white, or white with a few drops of the wall color. Otherwise the room can get too dark and feel boxy.)

Adding representation of your Taoist animal sign brings your animal symbol to life. I recommended that a client put two stuffed toys in her Earth/relationship that represented the animal signs of her and her partner. She was born in the year of the Serpent and her partner was born in the year of the Monkey. A little stuffed monkey and a cute stuffed snake now sit in permanent embrace on their bedroom dresser in the corner.

NINE

Lo P'an Compass
and I Ching

THE LUCK OF A LOCATION can be evaluated by using a magnetic *lo p'an* compass. *Lo* means "spiral" and *p'an* means "plate"; this compass is configured as a banded plate with a rounded bottom like a saucer. The eight trigrams, indicated on an inner band of the compass, are used by most modern feng shui practitioners. A complete lo p'an compass has as many as thirty-eight

LO P'AN COMPASS

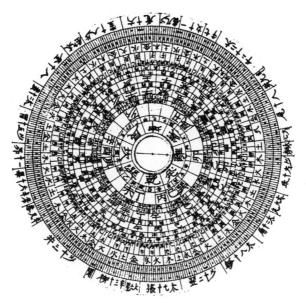

bands. The many bands provide extremely detailed information about all aspects of a location. This information is also influenced by the daily movements of the planets, as recorded in the *tong shu,* the Chinese farmer's almanac. The Duke of Zhou is credited with inventing the compass, although it may have been invented earlier in Chinese civilization. More than a thousand years later the use of the compass for feng shui became very highly developed during the Han dynasty.

The first (inner) band of the lo p'an compass depicts the eight trigrams of the early heaven sequence of the Taoist sage Fu Xi. Each trigram matches one of eight compass directions. Qian (Heaven) in the south is most yang. Kun (Earth) in the north is most yin. The movement from yang chi to yin chi and back again follows the changes of season. Note that south is always at the top of the Chinese compass.

The seasonal cycle of yang progressing to yin and back again is understood by observing the yearly cycle of the sun. The most yang time is the summer solstice, usually June 21 of the Gregorian calendar. Summer solstice is the longest day and the shortest night of the year. The most yin time is the winter

FU HSI'S EARLY HEAVEN SEQUENCE

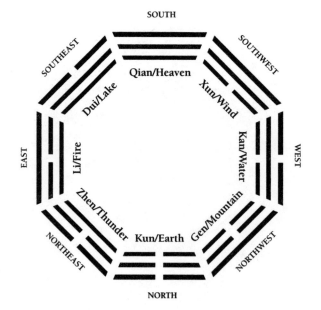

solstice, usually December 21 of the Gregorian calendar. Winter solstice is the shortest day and the longest night of the year. Yang and yin balance each other during the spring equinox and the autumn equinox. The spring equinox occurs on March 20 and the autumn equinox occurs around September 23 of the Gregorian calendar. On these two days, the day and night are of equal length on the planet earth. Seasonal yang chi and yin chi are in equilibrium.

Of the four dates that fall between the solstices and equinoxes, only one is widely celebrated in modern times. In ancient Europe, Lammas (also known as Lughnasad) was a crop festival that took place between the summer solstice and autumn equinox. Lammas was held on August 1 of the Gregorian calendar. Samhain (existing today as Halloween) is celebrated between the autumn equinox and winter solstice, on November 1. Imbolc (related to Candlemas) lies between the winter solstice and spring equinox, on February 1. Beltane (also known as May Day) occurs between the spring equinox and summer solstice, on May 1. The eight trigrams can be associated with the eight solar cycles, as illustrated in the diagram below.

THE EIGHT SOLAR CYCLES

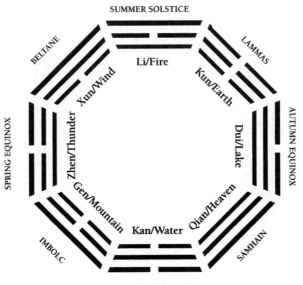

The Taoist cycle of yang progressing to yin and back again is manifest in the monthly cycle of the moon. The most yang time is during the full moon, when the sun's light is most fully reflected. The most yin time is during the new moon, when the sun's light is not reflected and darkness reigns. Yang and yin are in equilibrium during the first-quarter moon and the fourth-quarter moon phases, when half the moon is illuminated.

The four lunar phases between the full, new, and quarter moons are not as well known. The crescent moon is seen between the new moon and the first-quarter moon, the gibbous moon between the first-quarter and the full moon, the disseminating moon between the full moon and the fourth-quarter moon, and the balsamic moon between the fourth-quarter and the new moon. The eight trigrams can be associated with the eight lunar phases as illustrated in the following diagram.

THE EIGHT LUNAR PHASES

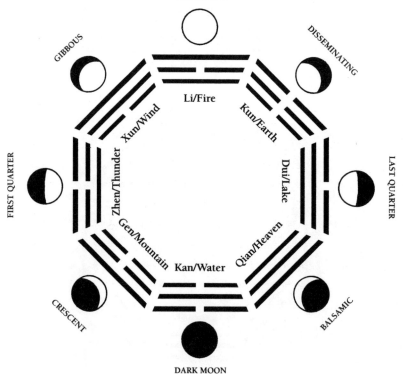

One band of the lo p'an compass depicts nine stars—the seven stars of the Big Dipper and two neighboring stars. The names of these nine stars translate as the breaker of armies, the military star, the literary star of cultural activities, the star of purity and truth, the star of the avaricious wolf, the star of official salary or rank preservation, the wide door or chief gate star, the left-hand assistant star, and the right-hand assistant star. They are also associated with formations of mountains and hills in the same way that the five elements are associated with landforms.

Another band of the compass illustrates the twenty-four solar terms. These divisions of the year are still used by farmers to assist them in planting during the agricultural year. They are important in feng shui because they indicate the patterns of movement of the earth's chi. Taoist astrologers observed the connection of the solar terms and the twelve branches to natural phenomena, especially the patterns of changes in chi of both earth and heaven together. The twelve earthly branches, lunar months, Gregorian dates, and Western astrological correlations are listed in the following chart.

LO P'AN AND WESTERN ASTROLOGY CORRELATES

EARTHLY Branch	LUNAR Month	SOLAR Terms	WESTERN Astrological sign
1st	11th	Great snow Dec. 7 and winter solstice Dec. 21	Sagittarius
2nd	12th	Slight cold Jan. 6 and great cold Jan. 26	Capricorn
3rd	1st	Beginning of spring Feb. 5 and rain water Feb. 19	Aquarius
4th	2nd	Waking of insects Mar. 5 and spring equinox Mar. 20	Pisces
5th	3rd	Clear and bright Apr. 5 and grain rain Apr. 20	Aries
6th	4th	Beginning of summer May 5 and grain full May 21	Taurus
7th	5th	Grain in ear June 2 and summer solstice June 21	Gemini
8th	6th	Slight heat July 7 and great heat July 23	Cancer
9th	7th	Beginning of autumn Aug. 7 and limit of heat Aug. 23	Leo
10th	8th	White dew Sept. 8 and autumn equinox Sept. 23	Virgo
11th	9th	Cold dew Oct. 8 and frost's descent Oct. 23	Libra
12th	10th	Beginning of winter Nov. 7 and slight snow Nov. 22	Scorpio

The ancient Taoists lived in harmony with seasonal cycles and the ecological changes in nature. Just as a serpent knows when to hibernate, and a pine tree knows when to produce sap, Chinese agrarian civilization lived in accordance with the solar terms. Modern life, with electric lights, climate-controlled buildings, and jet travel, can leave one disassociated from seasonal cycles that are in balance with the Tao and in balance with the principles of feng shui.

Other bands of the lo p'an compass illustrate the twelve animal signs of the Taoist zodiac. The twelve animals correspond to the following compass directions.

THE TWELVE ANIMAL SIGNS

Each of the twelve animals also correlates to two hours of each twenty-four-hour cycle. These hours are understood in conjunction with information from the Chinese farmer's almanac. It is most auspicious to make feng shui corrections associated with a particular sign during the hours ruled by that sign.

TWELVE ANIMALS CORRELATED TO TWENTY-FOUR HOUR CYCLE

11 P.M.–1 A.M.	Rat	11 A.M.–1 P.M.	Horse
1 A.M.–3 A.M.	Ox	1 P.M.–3 P.M.	Sheep
3 A.M.–5 A.M.	Tiger	3 P.M.–5 P.M.	Monkey
5 A.M.–7 A.M.	Hare	5 P.M.–7 P.M.	Phoenix
7 A.M.–9 A.M.	Dragon	7 P.M.–9 P.M.	Dog
9 A.M.–11 A.M.	Serpent	9 P.M.–11 P.M.	Boar

Yet another band of the compass indicates how the twelve animal signs are divided among the elements fire, metal, water, and wood. Fire animal signs are represented by the hot summer months: Serpent (May), Horse (June), and Sheep (July). Metal animal signs belong to autumn: Monkey (August), Phoenix (September), and Dog (October). Water animal signs are epitomized by the cold winter: Boar (November), Rat (December), and Ox (January). Wood animal signs are associated with spring: Tiger (February), Hare (March), and Dragon (April). All twelve signs are considered to be connected to the element earth and are referred to as the "twelve earthly branches."

Another band combines each one of the twelve earthly branches with one of the five elements, which creates a sixty-character cycle. This cycle designates successive days and years, as interpreted using the astrological information of the Chinese almanac. This sixty-character pattern multiplied by six creates the three hundred and sixty degrees of the ecliptic, the annual path of the sun.

The twelve animals are also divided into yang or yin types. Yang animals are Rat, Tiger, Dragon, Horse, Monkey, and Dog. Yin animals are Ox, Hare, Serpent, Sheep, Phoenix, and Boar.

Major lo p'an developments occurred during the northern Song dynasty (A.D. 960–1126), including the discovery of the significance of the ruling planets of the five elements in their nurturing, controlling, and reducing relationships. That information was added to the compass at this time. One of the five major planets rules each of the elements. Mars, the fiery red planet, rules fire; cold, hard Saturn rules earth; beautiful Venus rules metal; changeable Mercury rules water; and the largest planet, Jupiter, rules wood.

Many bands of the large lo p'an compass deal specifically with burial protocol. This is of great importance in China. A safe and ensure resting place for ancestors is valued because it is believed that they help and guide the living. The living provide the best burial possible to ensure that the deceased has an auspicious rebirth. An unpleasant burial site could affect the fortunes of the family for future generations. The correct burial site is of greatest importance for a royal person or a great sage.

Intensely thorough and sophisticated geomantic calculations are required to determine whether the chi of the land surrounding a tomb site is auspicious. There are dozens of angles of chi to consider, relating to roads, rivers, pathways, and chi movement at a tomb site. Assessment of the best direction for coffin and headstone placement is also vital, as is the angle at which the sun rises at the grave site. Astrological calculations are done for each site location, similar to what is known as horary astrology in the West. The compass rings depicting the "twelve palaces" (the Ming palace, brothers and sisters palace, marital palace, man and woman palace, wealth palace, health palace, moving palace, servants palace, officials palace, property palace, fortune and virtue palace, and parents palace) also play a significant part in astrology and in burial protocol. These "palaces" are similar to the "houses" of a Western horoscope. They indicate specific areas of life and family experience.

The outermost band of the lo p'an compass is unique because it is divided into portions of unequal size. This outermost band indicates the "mansions of the moon," the twenty-eight constellations through which the moon passes in its course along the ecliptic. The mansions, or resting places, of the moon were developed more than three thousand years ago and are documented in the Book of Rites. This outer band of the lunar orbit determines both general and specific lunar influences on a particular location aligned with the compass. Fifteen constellations are considered unlucky, and thirteen constellations are considered lucky. Important events, such as weddings, are planned during the most lucky periods.

Two compass rings depict hexagrams from the ancient Chinese book the I Ching, translated as the Book of Changes or the Classic of Change. The hexagrams on one compass ring indicate the present circumstance, and the hexa-grams on the next ring predict the future. A hexagram is created when two tri-grams are placed one above the other. The eight trigrams multiplied make sixty-four possible combinations. Each I Ching hexagram recommends proper con-duct for gaining good fortune or avoiding misfortune. Almost six hundred years after King Wen, toward the end of the Zhou dynasty, Confucius himself said in his old age, "If some years could be added to my life, I would give fifty of them to study the Book of Changes, for then I would have avoided great errors."

Casting the I Ching can help you develop your feng shui practice by offer-ing a further understanding of the eight trigram symbolism. Also, if you have a question about a specific feng shui procedure, you can consult the I Ching for an answer. Practical divination brings to life the truth of Heaven and Earth, which is also the truth of humanity, for we are part of the earth. Through the I Ching we can learn to accept cycles of change, as change is constant in nature. Ancient Taoist priests learned by observing nature, espe-cially topographic changes, to create feng shui. They realized that all things are in a continuous process of change.

The I Ching is the Taoist guide to comprehending cycles of change in nature and in life—the inevitable ebb and flow of circumstance, the waxing and waning of experience, and the growth and decay of activities. Through understanding and accepting change, Heaven can become one with human experience. We can honor continuous cycles of rising and falling chi, times of ill or good fortune, and learn to behave in harmony with universal forces, the will of Heaven.

Rolling with cycles is not easy for most westerners to accept. We often assume that we control our destiny through drive, will, and ambition, and that our fortunes will simply rise forever. While it is admirable to be responsible for one's actions and the resulting outcome, life cannot be lived in a constant yang state if one is to be balanced. At times there are cycles of inactivity, peri-ods of rest, that also need to be respected to maintain balance. The sun does not shine twenty-four hours a day. Nor is it dark day and night. There is a time for yang chi and a time for yin chi.

Through casting the I Ching you can be guided to the appropriate cycle of activity for your situation. Even if you do not like the answer that arises, that is the hexagram that speaks to your development at that time. Don't keep tossing coins until you finally receive the answer that you want. Accept what is revealed and meditate on its implications.

To cast the I Ching, begin with six coins, one of them different than the other five. (This easy method of I Ching divination was developed by the feng shui master Lin Yun Rinpoche.) For example, five dimes and a nickel will do. Shake the coins in your hand and form them in a stack in your palm. Then place the stack on your desk. Slide out the bottom coin. If the coin is heads up it is yang. Draw a solid yang line on a sheet of paper. If the coin is tails up it is yin. Draw a broken yin line on a sheet of paper. Slide the next coin from the bottom of the stack and draw the yang or yin line over the first line on your paper. Draw one more coin and line to create your first trigram.

Continue with the last three coins in the stack, from the bottom up, and draw either yin lines or yang lines to create the second trigram. This first hexagram indicates your present circumstance.

The one coin that differs from the other five, the nickel in the example, is called the "changing line" because in Taoism all things are in a constant state of flux. Redraw your hexagram and change the line that represents the nickel. If it was a yang line, redraw it as yin. If it was a yin line, redraw it as yang. This will create a new hexagram. This second hexagram predicts your future.

Find the upper and lower trigrams of your hexagrams on the following chart and match them to a number. The upper trigram, made of your last three coins, is found across the top of the chart. The lower trigram, made of your first three coins, is read in the column on the left of the chart. Match the number to the explanation on the following pages for a further understanding of your present and future.

Following is a simplified version of the I Ching to start you on the path of divination. For a more thorough understanding of this ancient oracle, I recommend *The Complete I Ching* by the Taoist master Alfred Huang.

Upper Trigram

	Qian	Zhen	Kan	Gen	Kun	Xun	Li	Dui
Qian	1	34	5	26	11	9	14	43
Zhen	25	51	3	27	24	42	21	17
Kan	6	40	29	4	7	59	64	47
Gen	33	62	39	52	15	53	56	31
Kun	12	16	8	23	2	20	35	45
Xun	44	32	48	18	46	57	50	28
Li	13	55	63	22	36	37	30	49
Dui	10	54	60	41	19	61	38	58

(Left side label: Lower Trigram)

☰ 1. Qian. Creative Energy. Heaven above. Heaven below.

This hexagram of heavenly essence represents healthy pure yang chi in action. It is direct energy, the big bang, the core of action. Initiate a new project and apply your powerful actions to follow the way of heaven. Create good works that benefit all humanity. In this way, you can achieve your goal and meet with success. This hexagram is especially exciting for those born in the year of the Dragon or Monkey.

☷ 2. Kun. Gentle Response. Earth above. Earth below.

This hexagram of earthly essence represents receptive, adaptive, nurturing energy, and the essence of pure yin chi. It is the yin balance to the preceding yang hexagram. Instead of direct action, just respond naturally and be open to receiving good fortune, as the gentle earth receives rain and sunshine. Meditation, inner peace, and mindful grace lead to attainment. Success is achieved through adaptability and connection to earth cycles. This hexagram is favorable for those born in the year of the Serpent.

☵☳ 3. Zhun. New Beginning. Water above. Thunder below.

In this hexagram chi is gathering, assembling, and perhaps struggling to take form. It can indicate challenging new beginnings, such as birth pangs, as one moves into the unknown. If there is not difficulty, the gathering and filling up of chi represents natural abundance. The unknown is merely a new form, like a sprout breaking from the seed. There is much potential for development.

☶☵ 4. Meng. Like a Child. Mountain above. Water below.

This hexagram is the inverse of the preceding one. After a new beginning, there is a situation of new experiences. You may not always know the correct way to proceed. Like a child, this is part of the cycle of growth and learning. A child's soul is like a piece of uncarved jade, ready to receive whatever is inscribed upon it. Cultivate a pure mind and heart like the pure water that flows from a mountain. This hexagram is a call to learn, grow, and achieve. You are the pupil and the way of the Tao, the essence of life, is the teacher.

☵☰ 5. Xu. Patiently Waiting. Water above. Heaven below.

This hexagram augers a cycle of patience and waiting, as if waiting for rain. All will come to you, but chi is still aligning and structuring until the time is ripe. There are needs to be met before further action is taken. Maintain faith and integrity of character while factors are still beyond your control.

☰☵ 6. Song. Possible Conflict. Heaven above. Water below.

This hexagram is the inverse of the preceding one. This is a warning to be aware that even though you are strongly on your path, there is potential for contention and conflict. Unseen obstacles can result in unfavorable outcome and negative reaction from others. It may be helpful to compromise, try to create balance, and quietly honor your experience of the truth. More planning is required.

☷☵ 7. Shi. The Power of an Army. Earth above. Water below.

This hexagram indicates how you are strengthened by the energy of the multitude, a collective force, as if empowered by an army. Discipline, organization, and the support of those around you are required to attain your goal. This collective action must be of the highest good for all involved.

☵☷ 8. Bi. Unity. Water above. Earth below.

This hexagram is the inverse of the preceding one. It augurs that in your endeavors now, of most importance is to honor your close relationships and value your intimate bonds. Bonding with another, a soulful connection, and unity of spirit are required to achieve your goal. Unity with others creates opportunities for both you and those close to you. This can extend to include your neighborhood and community. Also implied in this hexagram is to avoid union with the wrong people.

☴☰ 9. Xiao Xu. Small Gain. Wind above. Heaven below.

This hexagram augers that on your current course of action, it is best to hold back and restrain your energy because not much can be accumulated. There may be very little result from even your best efforts. This is not a good time to start a business or begin a new endeavor. In relationships remain polite and wait, or else gently separate. Instead of action, gather or store personal chi since plans and ideals are frustrated in their realization. It is as if the rain clouds are thick, but still there is no rain.

☰☱ 10. Lu. Proper Conduct. Heaven above. Lake below.

This hexagram, the inverse of the preceding one, indicates the importance of mindful behavior, of conducting yourself properly, walking carefully, speaking courteously, and fulfilling your duties with integrity. Sha chi cannot affect you if you conduct yourself with dignity and respect. Discernment is also required to avoid those who do not behave with dignity. In business transactions, behave with emotional maturity and do not lose your temper. Fulfill your agreements and behave with propriety and good manners to avoid problems and attain success. This advice is especially good for those born in the year of the Rat.

☷☰ 11. Tai. Peace and Prosperity. Earth above. Heaven below.

This hexagram of joy, bliss, and good fortune is like springtime, the first month of the Chinese New Year. Beauty surrounds you and there is opportunity for growth. Health is robust and you are secure. This is a good time to expand your social circle to create fruitful outcomes from interactions with others. Peace, benevolence, and prosperity are augured. There is positive advancement on your life journey.

☰☷ 12. Pi. Obstructions. Heaven above. Earth below.

This hexagram, the inverse of the preceding one, is the experience of misfortune and sorrow, which are the complements of bliss and joy. Hindrance, obstruction, and stagnation are now augered. Your good endeavors may be met with indifference or rejection. The weak and trivial is celebrated while the strong and creative is neglected. Do not follow, or attempt to lead, others. This is a time of decay or decadence; do not engage in it.

☰☲ 13. Tong Ren. Balance. Heaven above. Fire below.

This hexagram augers that there is peace and equality in the Middle Kingdom. Fortunate new endeavors benefit from the help of others. Solutions to challenges are attained through alliances. People behave harmoniously with one another in a sense of community.

☲☰ 14. Da Yu. Great Gain. Fire above. Heaven below.

This hexagram is the inverse of the preceding hexagram. It augers great good fortune, symbolized by an abundant harvest and possession of the ten thousand things. This is a time of extreme success. Remain mindful, humble, and gentle in your heart while you reap these rewards. This hexagram is especially appreciated by those born in the year of the Ox or Phoenix.

䷎ 15. Qian. Modest and Humble. Earth above. Mountain below.

Note that even though this hexagram has the same name as the first hexagram, they are composed of different characters. This hexagram augers that it is time to balance extremes. Moderation, equilibrium, and balance of the Tao are required for success. Extreme actions and thoughts lead to confusion. Instead modesty, humbleness, and gentleness are required. Behave with politeness, decorum, and courtesy. Cultivate the middle path of peace and stay centered.

䷏ 16. Yu. Contentment. Thunder above. Earth below.

This hexagram is the inverse of the preceding hexagram. It augers harmony and balance in the natural world, like beautifully composed music that brings delight and contentment. Your plans and projects receive the enthusiastic support of others. There is also a slight warning to not indulge excessively in pleasure.

䷐ 17. Sui. Follow. Lake above. Thunder below.

This hexagram augers that success is attained by mindfully following, adapting to, and agreeing with the restful cycle of life. This is not a time of courageous new endeavors. Instead, acquiesce and learn with a peaceful attitude. Understand your place in the situation and release control. Be flexible and let others lead.

䷑ 18. Gu. Time to Heal. Mountain above. Wind below.

This hexagram is the inverse of the preceding hexagram. It augers that inaction can become stagnation. That which is weak in your life can collapse, corrupt, and spoil. What is in a state of chaos and disarray requires time and work to remedy the situation. If you give much attention to details, focus your energy, organize, and correct past problems, success can be attained.

䷒ 19. Lin. Leadership. Earth above. Lake below.

This hexagram augers that this is your time of leadership, promotion, and authority. Pursue new goals and do not wait. Act swiftly with confidence. Luck will be yours. You will be rewarded for your progress.

≡≡ **20. Guan. Contemplation. Wind above. Earth below.**

This hexagram is the inverse of the preceding hexagram. It augers that success is achieved through watching, tending to, observing, examining, and contemplating your current situation. You can gather your power, develop foresight, and be able to journey forward wisely.

≡≡ **21. Shi He. Eradication. Fire above. Water below.**

This hexagram augers that you may be experiencing difficulties that require transformation to a higher level of consciousness. Cultivate truth and justice to eradicate or remove obstructions to harmony. Do what is realistically appropriate and do not go to extremes. There is also a slight warning to avoid bad companions who create mischief.

≡≡ **22. Bi. Grace. Mountain above. Fire below.**

This hexagram is the inverse of the preceding hexagram. It augers a time of grace, balance, and prosperity. You can possess an understanding of the beauty of the universe. Cultivate goodness and refine your surroundings with feng shui embellishments. Social life is stimulated, whereby success is attained through elegant conduct and appreciation of etiquette. There is a slight warning against artifice. This hexagram is especially fortunate for those born in the year of the Hare or Sheep.

≡≡ **23. Bo. Decline. Mountain above. Earth below.**

This hexagram augers that the beauty of the preceding hexagram has fallen away. Like the lunar cycle, after the full moon comes the waning moon. Your situation has reached its peak and is now starting to decline. Do not forge ahead or engage in social activities. Instead, remain calm, take care of yourself, and appreciate those closest to you.

≡≡ **24. Fu. Begin Again. Earth above. Thunder below.**

This hexagram is the inverse of the preceding hexagram. It augers the time of winter solstice, when yin chi is abundant yet yang chi begins to rise. It is time to begin again, return to the start, and create a new life cycle. You may be experiencing frustration and delay because an old cycle is ending. Success can be attained by contemplating the end and not acting rashly.

☰ 25. Wu Wang. Innocence. Heaven above. Thunder below.

This hexagram augers that a childlike innocence, the natural pure state of humans, is the best way to experience your current state of affairs. Cultivate an innocent, honest, and trustful attitude. Rely on your instinct and intuition, not cleverness and intrigue.

☶ 26. Da Xu. Great Good Fortune. Mountain above. Heaven below.

This hexagram is the inverse of the preceding hexagram. It augers great good fortune, accumulation of virtue, achievement, and the ability to direct your power. This is an excellent time to start a new business or open a new door of opportunity. You can have a positive and strong influence on others. There is a slight warning that you should avoid recklessness during this fortunate time of advancement. Integrity of character must be maintained, which leads to maturity.

☶ 27. Yi. Nourishment. Mountain above. Thunder below.

This hexagram is symbolic of the food that nourishes us. It is advised to eat a healthy, nutritious diet and eat in moderation. On another level, this hexagram is symbolic of spiritual nurturing of self and others. Pursue wisdom and love learning. Most important is to nurture your virtue.

☱ 28. Da Guo. Great Action. Lake above. Wind below.

This hexagram is the opposite of the preceding hexagram. It augers great nourishing and extraordinary action. When one is greatly nourished, extraordinary action can result. To advance is very favorable. There are many opportunities and possibilities. Much success can be achieved.

☵ 29. Kan. Cold, Dark, and Wet. Water above. Water below.

This is the hexagram of possible danger. An ancient form of this hexagram illustrates someone falling into a pit. The color of the element water is black, hence the association with darkness. Maintain confidence, faith, and virtue. In this way, one falls but is not drowned. One is in danger but not completely lost. This is not a time for action. To heedlessly plunge into a difficult situation will result in misfortune. This hexagram is especially important to heed for those born in the year of the Tiger or Horse, specifically the red fire Horse.

☲ 30. Li. Bright Success. Fire above. Fire below.

This hexagram is the opposite of the preceding hexagram. It represents pure fire and brightness after the darkness. This hexagram augers that your effectiveness and achievement can exceed expectations. It is also fortunate to work together with others. Individual effort as well as cooperative efforts can meet with much success.

☱ 31. Xian. Embrace. Lake above. Mountain below.

This hexagram augers a close relationship, possibly marriage. Attraction, perseverance, and finally attainment can occur. Now is the time to take the initiative. You have the advantage of inner strength. In your dealings, be stable as a mountain and as pure as the water in a lake. There will be reciprocity from others. You will be embraced.

☳ 32. Heng. Durability. Thunder above. Wind below.

This hexagram is the inverse of the preceding hexagram. After the symbolic marriage of the previous hexagram, the union should last a long time. Unselfishness, purity, sincerity, and mutual caring are necessary qualities for the relationship to endure. New goals can be attained with constancy of character. Traditions that endure do so because they have value.

☶ 33. Dun. Retreat. Heaven above. Mountain below.

This hexagram augers that it may not be fortunate to go forward with plans. Instead, it is a time of retreat, meditation, and contemplation of past actions until it is time to move forward. Do not fight for power. Stop, heal, and make your home a sacred place. Do not consider this defeat or abandonment, but wise acknowledgment of a futile situation.

䷡ 34. Da Zhuang. Great Strength. Thunder above. Heaven below.

This hexagram is the inverse of the preceding one. It augers that you may be in a leadership role. Your actions can influence others and you can attract much positive attention. Now is the time to go forth with your plans. Most important is to maintain virtue, integrity, and correct behavior. Your greatest strength is your strength of character.

䷢ 35. Jing. Swift Progress. Fire above. Earth below.

This hexagram augers powerful chi and advancement on your life path. You can meet with success and be rewarded for your achievements. Progress is swift and respect from others is forthcoming. Expand your social circle to receive support from others. There is a slight warning that to proceed too quickly without mindfulness can lead to regret.

䷣ 36. Ming Yi. Less Light. Earth above. Fire below.

This hexagram is the inverse of the preceding hexagram. It augers that it is best to wait, submit, and gently restrain your chi until circumstances change. You may not be in a powerful situation and forces that are not to your agreement may have the advantage. Behave with virtue and integrity of character, regardless of how you feel emotionally.

䷤ 37. Jia Ren. Home and Family. Wind above. Fire below.

This hexagram augers that domestic relationships are important at this time. Your intimate family unit can maintain their strong bond through mutual love, respect, and acceptance of responsibilities. Business and other relationships seem to be an extension of the family unit. Achieve a balance, behave not too sternly yet not too permissively.

䷥ 38. Kui. Diplomacy. Fire above. Lake below.

This hexagram is the inverse of the preceding hexagram. It augers that there may be opposing ideas about the current situation. Only small gains may be made at this time because there may not be unified support for mutual goals.

Avoid a battle of wills. Strive for understanding by diplomatically seeking common ground. Respect the opinions of others, even if they do not agree with your ideals.

䷦ 39. Jian. Challenges. Water above. Mountain below.

This hexagram augers possible difficulties and challenges on your path. There is no fault or blame. Hardship is part of life experience. Do not rush ahead, yet do not quit. Rest, retreat, and wait since it may take time to overcome hardship. Seeking counsel from others may be helpful, especially in business.

䷧ 40. Jie. Relief. Thunder above. Water below.

This hexagram, the inverse of the preceding one, augers that the time may be right to heal the past, move forward, and create positive change in your life. A sense of relief can result from releasing the past. Resolve social and personal complications. You are then ready for new growth and opportunity.

䷨ 41. Sun. Simplify. Mountain above. Lake below.

This hexagram augers that it may be time to simplify your life. Decrease your possessions and live economically. Then you may realistically appreciate life and not be deluded by consumerist fantasy. You may benefit from the sacrifices that you chose to make. In business, financial gain may be little so reorganize and restructure.

䷩ 42. Yi. Advancement. Wind above. Thunder below.

This hexagram is the inverse of the preceding hexagram. It augers that now may be a time of opportunity and advancement. Even large difficulties may be easier to overcome. Goals can be attained but it is best to act swiftly. If you are in a position of power, serve and assist others so they too may gain and increase their good fortune.

䷪ 43. Guai. Integrity. Lake above. Heaven below.

This hexagram augers that firm resolve, dedication to truth, and high integrity of character may be required to achieve your goals. You cannot compromise. You must remove negative, evil, and inferior influences from your life. Do not hesitate or avoid this necessary transformation. In dealing with others, demonstrate positive behavior and do not dwell on their faults.

☰ 44. Gou. New Encounters. Heaven above. Wind below.

This hexagram is the inverse of the preceding hexagram. This hexagram augers that you may meet a person or people in an unexpected encounter. It is necessary to know them well and work together only for the highest good. Otherwise, consider this hexagram a warning because the truth may be veiled. An unworthy person may connive to receive your favors. Do not be deluded by glamour or tempted into schemes that lack integrity.

☱ 45. Cui. Coming Together. Lake above. Earth below.

This hexagram augers that people may come together for a common purpose. They may share a common belief, or perhaps they share a common ancestry. Maintain strong bonds through trustful and sincere interactions. You can trust the leader and have access to speak with him or her. If you are the leader, make sure that the group is secure and maintains their common purpose.

☷ 46. Sheng. Great Growth. Earth above. Wind below.

This hexagram is the inverse of the preceding one. It augers advancement and growth beyond expectations. You can experience much personal power, esteem, respect, even fame at this time. This is the result of your hard work over a period of time. Do not waver or retreat. Be assertive and confident to sustain your good luck. You can approach those in positions of authority. This may also be an opportune time to seek a mentor or teacher.

☱ 47. Kun. Exhaustion. Lake above. Water below.

This hexagram is perhaps the most challenging of all sixty-four hexagrams. It augers a time of difficulty, hardship, exhaustion, even poverty. There is little opportunity for growth. Instead there is confinement and oppression. Communication may be misunderstood. Accept your situation and examine your motives. Remain patient and steady. Do not indulge in melancholia or anger.

≣ **48. Jing. Replenish. Water above. Wind below.**

This hexagram is the inverse of the preceding hexagram. It augers that it may be wise to take care of yourself, rest, and heal. Replenish with long baths and nutritious meals. Sleep extra hours and dream to release psychological emotions. Once you have rested, you can pursue your goals.

≣ **49. Ge. Shed the Old. Lake above. Fire below.**

This hexagram augers that your stagnant situation may require transformation. Now is the time to abolish the old and bring in the new and better. Strive for clarity of purpose to make progress and implement improvements. Perhaps request the opinions of others to determine what best benefits the common good. Avoid haste and excess because mindfulness is required to make these changes.

≣ **50. Ding. New Opportunities. Fire above. Wind below.**

This hexagram is the inverse of the preceding hexagram. It augers that success can be achieved at this time. Pursue new opportunities which bring good fortune. You possess an understanding of the events taking place. Rely on those with experience to offer guidance. Family and friends can also be helpful.

≣ **51. Zhen. Thunderstorm. Thunder above. Thunder below.**

This hexagram augers an explosion of energy like springtime thunderstorms that awaken new life. What may start boldly or shockingly can become successful and prosperous. Now is the time to take fast action and start a new cycle of activity. Maintain your composure and inner strength. Be sure to thoroughly complete all transactions begun at this time so as not to block further advancement.

≣ **52. Gen. Still As a Mountain. Mountain above. Mountain below.**

This hexagram is the inverse of the preceding hexagram. It augers that events cannot continue at a rapid pace. A key to success is to know when it is time to keep still and when it is time to advance. Now may be time to keep still, stop, rest, and seek inner peace. Try not to mentally race ahead with plans and goals, especially concerning relationships. A quiet mind, honesty, and sincerity bring good fortune.

䷴ 53. Jian. Balanced Development. Wind above. Mountain below.

This hexagram augers to go forward but to do so in a slow, orderly way. Progress is made step by step. Calmly follow the correct sequence of events to attain good fortune. Do not agitate or expect rapid gain. Do not madly follow passions. Instead, stay firm on your path and cultivate patience.

䷵ 54. Gui Mei. Imbalanced Relationship. Thunder above. Lake below.

This hexagram is the inverse of the preceding hexagram. It augers imbalance in relationships whereby you may be in the subordinate position. Your contributions may not be valued or required. Your sincere communication is misunderstood. As difficult as it may seem, it is best to be passive and not attract attention. It is not favorable to assert your will. Stay focused on your long-range plan, but do not attempt to implement any actions at this time.

䷶ 55. Feng. Great Abundance. Thunder above. Fire below.

This hexagram augers great abundance, success, and recognition. Share your abundance with those who helped you achieve it. Enjoy your good fortune yet maintain clarity of mind and focus of purpose. Wisely understand that this period of abundance will not last forever, so remain humble.

䷷ 56. Lu. Expansion. Fire above. Mountain below.

This hexagram is the inverse of the preceding hexagram. It augers a time to move forward and begin a new life cycle. You may try new things, but little seems to take solid root. Relationships may be transitory so do not assume that they will lead to serious commitments. Do not make long-range plans or seek overwhelming goals. Instead stay steadfast and upright while you explore new opportunities. Avoid decadence. There is also indication to not dwell on trivial things.

☴ 57. Xun. Gentle and Humble. Wind above. Wind below.

This hexagram augers that success is attained by being like the gentle wind. In China a gentle breeze with bright sun or a gentle breeze with mild rain is considered to be the best weather. The wind penetrates everywhere and is best when gentle. You too can influence others and penetrate everywhere, but remain gentle and humble to gain their support. Be clear and consistent. Extreme measures are not advised. Instead, patience and commitment are required.

☱ 58. Dui. Much Joy. Lake above. Lake below.

This hexagram augers the joy of giving and receiving. Your social life may be vibrant. Maintain a kind, positive, and very supportive attitude now if you are popular and others are loyal to you. This is not the time for criticism. Behave outwardly in a gentle manner but stay strong and firm in your resolve. There is also a slight warning against artifice and unrealistic optimism.

☴ 59. Huan. Scattered. Wind above. Water below.

This hexagram augers that focus may become scattered. To avoid this, now is the time to come together in spirit. Understand that which divides us from each other must be overcome to attain a common good and service to humanity. Do not judge others as better or worse than yourself. Strive to relate to all people as equals.

☵ 60. Jie. Boundaries. Water above. Lake below.

This hexagram augers setting boundaries and understanding limitations. Thrift and economy are important at this time. Restrain your energy in business affairs also. Strive for a balance between excess and deficiency. This is not time for emotional or passionate extremes. Walk the middle path. In this way you will not experience a flood, nor will you experience a drought.

䷼ 61. Zhong Fu. Sincerity. Wind above. Lake below.

This hexagram augers that sincerity, trustworthiness, honesty, and reliability can lead to great fortune and attainment of goals. Sincerity and trustworthiness are the cornerstones of good character. In this way, you can fulfill your obligations with ease and confidence. Do not engage in any type of vain, coarse, or decadent behavior.

䷽ 62. Xiao Guo. Small Interactions. Thunder above. Mountain below.

This hexagram augers that it is best not to overreach. Powerful endeavors may not be favored at this time. Great affairs should not be dealt with because you may not be ready. Instead, behave very mindfully, consciously, and attentively in even the smallest interactions with others. Cultivate dignity of character. Do not overspend; avoid extremes. It is better to go too slow than to go too fast.

䷾ 63. Ji Ji. Goals Fulfilled. Water above. Fire below.

This hexagram augers that perfect balance and harmony can be attained. Achievements and obligations can be very successfully fulfilled. This is a time of climax. Yet after achieving goals, you can lose focus and become lax. Even worse is to want more success and become greedy. Don't let your path that finally results in good fortune become chaotic when goals are attained.

䷿ 64. Wei Ji. The Future. Fire above. Water below.

This hexagram is the inverse of the preceding hexagram. It augers that a new beginning may be challenging. Therefore create order out of disorder and success out of confusion. Do not be weak and foolishly overextend. There is opportunity for the future. A journey of ten thousand miles begins from where you now stand.

Lunar Calendar from 1900 to 2032

(Note which years are "blind.")

1900—January 31 to February 18, 1901	white metal Rat
1901—February 19 to February 7, 1902	silver metal Ox
1902—February 8 to January 28, 1903	black water Tiger
1903—January 29 to February 15, 1904	gray water Hare
1904—February 16 to February 3, 1905	green wood Dragon
1905—February 4 to January 24, 1906	blue wood Serpent
1906—January 25 to February 12, 1907	red fire Horse
1907—February 13 to February 1, 1908	purple fire Sheep
1908—February 2 to January 21, 1909	yellow earth Monkey
1909—January 22 to February 9, 1910	gold earth Phoenix
1910—February 10 to January 29, 1911	white metal Dog
1911—January 30 to February 17, 1912	silver metal Boar
1912—February 18 to February 5, 1913	black water Rat
1913—February 6 to January 25, 1914	gray water Ox
1914—January 26 to February 13, 1915	green wood Tiger
1915—February 14 to February 2, 1916	blue wood Hare
1916—February 3 to January 22, 1917	red fire Dragon
1917—January 23 to February 10, 1918	purple fire Serpent

1918—February 11 to January 31, 1919	yellow earth Horse
1919—February 1 to February 19, 1920	gold earth Sheep
1920—February 20 to February 7, 1921	white metal Monkey
1921—February 8 to January 27, 1922	silver metal Phoenix
1922—January 28 to February 15, 1923	black water Dog
1923—February 16 to February 4, 1924	gray water Boar
1924—February 5 to January 24, 1925	green wood Rat
1925—January 25 to February 12, 1926	blue wood Ox
1926—February 13 to February 1, 1927	red fire Tiger
1927—February 2 to January 22, 1928	purple fire Hare
1928—January 23 to February 9, 1929	yellow earth Dragon
1929—February 10 to January 29, 1930	gold earth Serpent
1930—January 30 to February 16, 1931	white metal Horse
1931—February 17 to February 5, 1932	silver metal Sheep
1932—February 6 to January 25, 1933	black water Monkey
1933—January 26 to February 13, 1934	gray water Phoenix
1934—February 14 to February 3, 1935	green wood Dog
1935—February 4 to January 23, 1936	blue wood Boar
1936—January 24 to February 10, 1937	red fire Rat
1937—February 11 to January 30, 1938	purple fire Ox
1938—January 31 to February 18, 1939	yellow earth Tiger
1939—February 19 to February 7, 1940	gold earth Hare
1940—February 8 to January 26, 1941	white metal Dragon
1941—January 27 to February 14, 1942	silver metal Serpent
1942—February 15 to February 4, 1943	black water Horse
1943—February 5 to January 24, 1944	gray water Sheep
1944—January 25 to February 12, 1945	green wood Monkey
1945—February 13 to February 1, 1946	blue wood Phoenix
1946—February 2 to January 21, 1947	red fire Dog
1947—January 22 to February 9, 1948	purple fire Boar
1948—February 10 to January 28, 1949	yellow earth Rat
1949—January 29 to February 16, 1950	gold earth Ox
1950—February 17 to February 5, 1951	white metal Tiger

1951—February 6 to January 26, 1952	silver metal Hare
1952—January 27 to February 13, 1953	black wood Dragon
1953—February 14 to February 2, 1954	gray wood Serpent
1954—February 3 to January 23, 1955	green wood Horse
1955—January 24 to February 11, 1956	blue wood Sheep
1956—February 12 to January 30, 1957	red fire Monkey
1957—January 31 to February 17, 1958	purple fire Phoenix
1958—February 18 to February 7, 1959	yellow earth Dog
1959—February 8 to January 27, 1960	gold earth Boar
1960—January 28 to February 14, 1961	white metal Rat
1961—February 15 to February 4, 1962	silver metal Ox
1962—February 5 to January 24, 1963	black water Tiger
1963—January 25 to February 12, 1964	gray water Hare
1964—February 13 to February 1, 1965	green wood Dragon
1965—February 2 to January 20, 1966	blue wood Serpent
1966—January 21 to February 8, 1967	red fire Horse
1967—February 9 to January 29, 1968	purple fire Sheep
1968—January 30 to February 16, 1969	yellow earth Monkey
1969—February 17 to February 5, 1970	gold earth Phoenix
1970—February 6 to January 26, 1971	white metal Dog
1971—January 27 to February 15, 1972	silver metal Boar
1972—February 16 to February 2, 1973	black water Rat
1973—February 3 to January 22, 1974	gray water Ox
1974—January 23 to February 10, 1975	green wood Tiger
1975—February 11 to January 30, 1976	blue wood Hare
1976—January 31 to February 17, 1977	red fire Dragon
1977—February 18 to February 6, 1978	purple fire Serpent
1978—February 7 to January 27, 1979	yellow earth Horse
1979—January 28 to February 15, 1980	gold earth Sheep
1980—February 16 to February 4, 1981	white metal Monkey
1981—February 5 to January 24, 1982	silver metal Phoenix
1982—January 25 to February 12, 1983	black water Dog
1983—February 13 to February 1, 1984	gray water Boar

1984—February 2 to February 1, 1985	green wood Rat
1985—February 2 to February 8, 1986	blue wood Ox
1986—February 9 to January 28, 1987	red fire Tiger
1987—January 29 to February 16, 1988	purple fire Hare
1988—February 17 to February 15, 1989	yellow earth Dragon
1989—February 16 to January 26, 1990	gold earth Serpent
1990—January 27 to February 14, 1991	white metal Horse
1991—February 15 to February 3, 1992	silver metal Sheep
1992—February 4 to January 22, 1993	black water Monkey
1993—January 23 to February 9, 1994	gray water Phoenix
1994—February 10 to January 30, 1995	green wood Dog
1995—January 31 to February 18, 1996	blue wood Boar
1996—February 19 to February 6, 1997	red fire Rat
1997—February 7 to January 27, 1998	purple fire Ox
1998—January 28 to February 15, 1999	yellow earth Tiger
1999—February 16 to February 4, 2000	gold earth Hare
2000—February 5 to January 23, 2001	white metal Dragon
2001—January 24 to February 11, 2002	silver metal Serpent
2002—February 12 to January 31, 2003	black water Horse
2003—February 1 to January 21, 2004	gray water Sheep
2004—January 22 to February 8, 2005	green wood Monkey
2005—February 9 to January 28, 2006	blue wood Phoenix
2006—January 29 to February 17, 2007	red fire Dog
2007—February 18 to February 6, 2008	purple fire Boar
2008—February 7 to January 25, 2009	yellow earth Rat
2009—January 26 to February 13, 2010	gold earth Ox
2010—February 14 to February 2, 2011	white metal Tiger
2011—February 3 to January 22, 2012	silver metal Hare
2012—January 23 to February 9, 2013	black water Dragon
2013—February 10 to January 30, 2014	gray water Serpent
2014—January 31 to February 18, 2015	green wood Horse
2015—February 19 to February 7, 2016	blue wood Sheep
2016—February 8 to January 27, 2017	red fire Monkey

2017—January 28 to February 15, 2018	purple fire Phoenix
2018—February 16 to February 4, 2019	yellow earth Dog
2019—February 5 to January 24, 2020	gold earth Boar
2020—January 25 to February 11, 2021	white metal Rat
2021—February 12 to January 31, 2022	silver metal Ox
2022—February 1 to January 21, 2023	black water Tiger
2023—January 22 to February 9, 2024	gray water Hare
2024—February 10 to January 28, 2025	green wood Dragon
2025—January 29 to February 16, 2026	blue wood Serpent
2026—February 17 to February 5, 2027	red fire Horse
2027—February 6 to January 25, 2028	purple fire Sheep
2028—January 26 to February 12, 2029	yellow earth Monkey
2029—February 13 to February 1, 2030	gold earth Phoenix
2030—February 2 to January 22, 2031	white metal Dog
2031—January 23 to February 10, 2032	silver metal Boar

Feng Shui Resources

To contact the author:

Susan Levitt
c/o Destiny Books
One Park Street
Rochester, Vermont 05767
e-mail: susanlevitt@taofengshui.com
www.taofengshui.com

Lunar calendars can be ordered from:

We'Moon Lunar Calendars
Mother Tongue Ink
P.O. Box 1395–A
Estacada, Oregon 97023
Phone: 503-630-7848
e–mail: wemoon@teleport.com
www.teleport.com/~wemoon

Celestial Guide
Quicksilver Publications
P.O. Box 340, Dept. GK99
Ashland, Oregon 97520
Phone: 541-482-5342
Fax: 541-482-0960

Feng shui products can be ordered from:

Feng Shui Warehouse
P.O. Box 6689
San Diego, California 92166-0689
Phone: 1-800-399-1599 and 619-523-2158
e-mail: fengshuiwh@aol.com
www.fengshuiwarehouse.com

Gone with the Wind Chimes
1957 86th Street Suite 108
Brooklyn, New York 11214
Phone: 718-256-8773
Fax: 718-232-8054

Feng shui magazines:

Feng Shui Journal
P.O. Box 6689
San Diego, California 92166-0689
Phone: 1-800-399-1599 and 619-523-2158
e-mail: fengshuiwh@aol.com
www.fengshuiwarehouse.com

Feng Shui for Modern Living
Centennial Publishing
1st Floor, 1–5 Clerkenwell Road
London EC1M 5PA, United Kingdom
Phone: +44-(0) 171-251 0777
Fax: +44-(0) 171-251 5490
www.fengshui–magazine.com
e-mail: info@fengshui–magazine.com